150 Best Cupcake Recipes

150 Best Cupcake Recipes

Julie Hasson

Robert
ROSE

Design & Production: Kevin Cockburn/PageWave Graphics Inc.
Editor: Carol Sherman
Recipe Tester: Jennifer MacKenzie
Copy Editors: Christina Anson Mine and Karen Campbell-Sheviak
Cover Photography: Colin Erricson
Interior Photography: Mark T. Shapiro and Colin Erricson
Cover Food Styling: Kathryn Robertson
Interior Food Styling: Kate Bush and Kathryn Robertson
Props Styling: Charlene Erricson

Additional photography:
Assorted Cupcakes (Chocolate): © iStockphoto.com/YinYang
Mocha Cupcakes: © iStockphoto.com/Lauri Patterson
Mint Chocolate Cupcakes: © iStockphoto.com/Kelly Cline
Pink Lemonade Cupcakes: © iStockphoto.com/Ruth Black
Carrot Cupcakes: © iStockphoto.com/Stacey Newman
Assorted Cupcakes (Pink): © iStockphoto.com/Georgina Palmer

Cover image: Best Chocolate Cupcakes (page 18), White Cupcakes (page 85) and Lemon Yogurt Cupcakes (page 45)

We acknowledge the financial support of the Government of Canada through the Book Publishing Industry Development Program (BPIDP) for our publishing activities.

Published by Robert Rose Inc.
120 Eglinton Avenue East, Suite 800, Toronto, Ontario, Canada M4P 1E2
Tel: (416) 322-6552 Fax: (416) 322-6936
www.robertrose.ca

Printed in Canada

1 2 3 4 5 6 7 8 9 TG|LBF 20 19 18 17 16 15 14 13 12

Contents

Acknowledgments. 7

Introduction 8

    Decorating Tips and Techniques 9

    Theme Decorating. 9

    Simple Garnishes 10

    Decorating for Kids. 11

    Tools and Equipment 11

    Common Ingredients. 12

Chocolate. 17

Fruit 29

Nuts. 47

Adults Only. 59

Kids' Corner 75

Spice It Up 89

New Twists. 105

Vegan 125

Frostings, Glazes and Fillings 147

Sources 185

Index 186

Acknowledgments

I want to thank everyone involved with putting this book together. A big thank you to my agent, Lisa Ekus. Thank you, Bob Dees, for having the "cupcake vision." Thank you, Carol Sherman, for making everything come together so beautifully. Thanks, Jennifer MacKenzie for your excellent recipe testing, and Christina Anson Mine and Karen Campbell-Sheviak for their sharp copy editing. Thanks also to Mark Shapiro and Colin Erricson for the fine photography, Kate Bush and Kathryn Robertson for food styling, and Charlene Erricson for props styling. Thanks to Kevin Cockburn and everyone at PageWave Graphics. Thank you to everyone at Robert Rose for doing such a great job on this book!

I want to give a huge thank you to my incredible and awesome husband, Jay, who not only helped me put this book together, tested recipes and offered his poetic prose but also picked up all the pieces while I was in my cupcake zone. You're the best! Thank you, Sydney and Noah, my super cool kids, for eating cupcakes for breakfast, lunch and dinner and never complaining.

Thank you, Mom, for sharing your love of food with us. Thank you, Jon, for suggesting that I write a book on cupcakes. Thank you also to my wonderful crew of recipe and taste testers: Meredith Levin, Kelly Cavalier, Hannah Sowd, Stefanie Amann, Debyi Kucera and Kerstin Kraasch.

Introduction

Cupcakes are the perfect dessert. They can be savored privately or shared enthusiastically. They can be dressed up as a wedding cake or neatly tucked into a lunch box. And it doesn't matter if you're four or 40 — cupcakes are fun and delicious.

Then there's the subject of beauty. You have to admire the splendor of cupcakes. They are delectable miniature cakes with soft interiors, tapered sides and sweet frosting crowns. And the flavor combinations for both cake and frosting are limited only by your imagination.

While writing this book, I baked a mammoth number of cupcakes. As I ventured out to my neighbors' homes — feeling a lot like Donna Reed as I carried huge trays of cupcakes — I heard a frequent and familiar question: "What makes a cupcake a cupcake and not a muffin? They look the same." It's a good question, and I answered without hesitation. A muffin is dense and hearty and doesn't have a frosting. A cupcake, on the other hand, is light and cakelike, and is usually topped with a mound of frosting or a drizzle of icing.

As far as I'm concerned, cupcakes are delightful and not just for their versatility. They remind us of childhood, when we could eat a whole cupcake and not have to share. As adults, we can eat the whole thing and feel satisfied without guilt or calories (not too many, anyway!). Is it any wonder that cupcakes are making a timely resurgence into our homes and local bakeries? It's because they're adored by all. And, as I said, they're the perfect dessert.

— *Julie Hasson*

Decorating Tips and Techniques

How to frost a cupcake

There are two basic styles or techniques for topping your cupcakes with frosting.

Rustic cupcakes: This technique lends your cupcakes a homey elegance. There are several ways to achieve this easy look. The first is to simply top cooled cupcakes with a dollop of freshly whipped sweetened cream. The next is to use a small offset spatula, a butter knife or the back of a spoon to swirl a dollop of frosting decoratively around the top of the cupcake. Another technique is to place a dollop of frosting on top of the cupcake and, using a small offset spatula or butter knife, spread the frosting over the top to the edges, making the surface smooth and flat.

Fancy cupcakes: Cupcakes can also be frosted using a pastry bag and tip, creating elegant-looking cupcakes with eye appeal. To use this technique, you'll need a pastry bag fitted with a tip (and coupler, if your pastry bag comes with one). Place the pastry bag, tip end down, in a cup or glass with the top of the bag folded over the side of the cup or glass. Spoon frosting into the bottom of the bag. Lift up the top of the bag and twist it so that it forces the frosting into the bottom of the bag and out the tip. To hold the pastry bag, place the twisted part of the bag in the space between your thumb and forefinger. It's important to apply pressure using your entire hand. Start piping icing decoratively around the top of the cupcake.

For a simple pattern, use a fluted tip to pipe the frosting into a swirled peak on the top of the cupcake. You can also use a fluted tip to create a series of connected dots or rosettes on the top of the cupcake or use a medium-size plain tip to create polka dots.

Serve the cupcakes this way or garnish them further with sprinkles, colorful candies or chocolate shavings. A sharp vegetable peeler works very well for making chocolate shavings.

Theme Decorating

Valentine's Day

Pipe or spread the top of a cupcake with Easy Buttercream Frosting (page 159) and decorate with little candy hearts. Another great Valentine-themed idea cupcake is to top cupcakes with pink-tinted Easy Buttercream Frosting and a red gummy heart in the center.

Easter

Pipe or spread the top of a cupcake with Easy Buttercream Frosting (page 159). Sprinkle flaked coconut that has been tinted light green (like grass) over frosting. Arrange a couple of jelly beans on top to resemble Easter eggs in the coconut grass. A piece of licorice finishes off the top of the cupcake, resembling an Easter basket handle.

Halloween

Place half a rectangular or oblong cookie upright into the topping to look like a headstone for a graveyard effect.

Christmas

A simple look for Christmas is to frost your cupcakes with Easy Buttercream Frosting (page 159) and center a miniature candy cane on top. Alternatively, using a pastry bag, pipe green holly leaves on top of the white frosting. Place a few small red candies in a cluster in the center to look like berries.

Hanukkah

Top cupcakes with white or very light blue-tinted Easy Buttercream Frosting (page 159). Center a stencil of the Star of David over tops of cupcakes and dust with blue sprinkles or decorating sugar.

Weddings

A fun and popular alternative to a traditional wedding cake is to stack cupcakes on plastic tiers to resemble a large cake.

Birthdays

Here's a great way to say "Happy Birthday": on the top of each of 13 cupcakes, pipe one letter of the words "happy birthday."

Artsy

Pipe or spread the top of a cupcake with a white frosting, such as Easy Buttercream Frosting (page 159), Cream Cheese Icing (page 158) or Vanilla Cream Frosting (page 160). Then splatter tops of frosted cupcakes with melted chocolate, Jackson Pollock–style. Another great look is to pipe or spread the top of a cupcake with Easy Buttercream Frosting, then place round colored candies, such as M&M's, Smarties or Necco wafers, over top to achieve a polka-dot look.

Simple Garnishes

Here's a list of garnishes that all look great on frosted cupcakes.

Birthday candles

Colorful birthday candles work well on top of cupcakes. Look for both the short birthday candles and the tall, French-made birthday candles at supermarkets and kitchenware stores.

Dragées

These edible silver-color balls look decorative and festive on the tops of cupcakes.

Edible glitter

Here's a fun way to add edible sparkle to your cupcakes. Edible glitter is available in specialty stores and online, and it comes in a variety of colors. It's especially striking sprinkled on top of a white frosting, such as Easy Buttercream Frosting (page 159), Cream Cheese Icing (page 158) or Vanilla Cream Frosting (page 160).

Fresh berries

Sprinkle fresh berries over fluffy whipped cream.

Toasted chopped nuts

Toast nuts to bring out their fullest flavor. (To toast nuts, see page 14.)

Shards of nut brittle or toffee

Shards of nut brittle or toffee placed upright in the frosting give cupcakes an artsy appeal.

Edible fresh flowers

Look in your garden or specialty markets for edible flowers. (Make sure that they have not been sprayed with pesticides and that they are safe to eat.) Edible flowers have a simple and elegant look. Sprinkle petals or whole flowers over frosted cupcakes or place a single bloom in the center of the cupcake. Look for roses, lavender, violets, marigolds and orange blossoms.

Candied flower petals

Available in some specialty kitchen stores, candied rose petals and violets make stylish decorations.

Food coloring

Commonly available in liquid (in those little tiny tubes in most supermarkets), gel and paste forms, food coloring will tint white frosting, such as Easy Buttercream Frosting (page 159). Be careful to use only a small amount of the gel or paste types because these colors are very bright and strong, and a little goes a long way. I like to use a toothpick dipped in the color to tint a frosting.

Sprinkles and colored sugars

Look for these in the baking aisles of supermarkets and kitchenware stores. They look glittery sprinkled on top of frosted cupcakes, whether you use a heavy or a light hand.

Decorating for Kids

Top frosted cupcakes with toy cars or small plastic action figures, plastic palm trees or miniature plastic dolls. Teddy bear graham crackers or animal crackers work well, too, especially when placed upright on top of the frosting. They resemble circus or zoo animals. Miniature marshmallows, candies (such as gummy worms, gummy bears, Smarties, small button candies, etc.) look great on frosted cupcakes. Place Smarties decoratively on top to resemble colored polka dots.

Tools and Equipment

Muffin pans

The recipes in this book use a standard-size muffin pan (not the extra-large "Texas-size" variety). You can usually find these pans in grocery and kitchen stores. Look for heavier muffin pans with nonstick coating and 12 wells in them so you can bake a whole batch in one pan. It's also a good idea to have a few 6-cup muffin pans for recipes that make 18.

Shaped pans

Look for muffin pans with different-shaped wells in them for those times that you want to try something unique. I've seen pans with wells in the shape of stars, hearts and mini-brioches at kitchen stores and online.

Cupcake liners

Paper liners: These grease-resistant paper baking cups are available in the baking aisle of the supermarket. They come in white, pastels and holiday prints.

Foil liners: Although I primarily use paper liners, there are a few occasions on which I feel that foil liners are preferable. I tend to use them for recipes that are moist, such as cheesecake cupcakes, or for recipes that might stick to the paper liners, such as angel food cupcakes.

Baking equipment

Silicone baking pans: These are the baking pans of the future. They are made with food-safe silicone and can withstand temperatures from −140°F (−95°C) to 480°F (248°C). My favorite are Flexipans® from Demarle. They require no greasing and are totally nonstick.

Cooling rack: A cooling rack elevates a baking pan or baked goods so that air can circulate around them.

Dry measuring cups: These are the most accurate way to measure dry ingredients (with the exception of a digital scale). I like to use a good-quality set of measuring cups that nest and come in a variety of measurements. When measuring, always remember to scoop your dry ingredients into the cup and level the top by scraping across with the flat side of a knife or skewer. This will give you an accurate measurement.

Decorating tools

Offset spatula: Also referred to as a small angled icing spatula, this small spatula with an angled blade is made of flexible stainless steel and is perfect for spreading frosting over cupcakes. It gives you more control than a butter knife or spoon.

Pastry bag: Look for lightweight pastry bags that are strong and made from washable polyester. The lightweight bags are also coated to prevent any absorption or seepage of the grease from the fat in the frosting. They can be used over and over and still stay flexible. You can also find disposable bags made of clear plastic, which you can throw away when the decorating is done.

Pastry tips: There are many different pastry tips available for different effects, from star tips for making rosettes to writing tips for making straight lines or words.

Coupler: This two-part attachment fits on the tip of a pastry bag, enabling you to interchange several decorating tips without changing the bag.

Common Ingredients

Chocolate

Bittersweet, semisweet and unsweetened chocolates vary depending on the percentage of chocolate liquor (a by-product of the manufacturing of the cocoa beans into chocolate) and sugar they contain. By law, bittersweet and semisweet chocolates must contain at least 35% chocolate liquor.

Store chocolate in a cool, dry place for up to one year. Chocolate will sometimes develop a white "bloom," or coating, when it gets too warm, causing the cocoa butter to separate. The chocolate is still fine to use in recipes or for melting.

To melt chocolate in a microwave oven: In a large microwave-safe bowl (preferably a large glass measuring cup), melt chocolate (and cream or butter, if using) on High, uncovered, for 30-second intervals (stirring every 30 seconds) until melted and smooth. Be careful not to overheat or cook the chocolate too long, as it can easily burn.

I have tested the recipes in this book using a 1,000-watt microwave oven.

Bittersweet chocolate: This is a dark chocolate that contains less sugar than semisweet chocolate, with an intense flavor.

Semisweet chocolate: Semisweet chocolate is slightly sweeter, with a slightly less-intense chocolate flavor. Oftentimes, but not always, this chocolate can be used interchangeably with bittersweet chocolate.

Chocolate chips: Use good-quality, real semisweet chocolate chips. The better the quality, the better the taste of the final product.

White chocolate: White chocolate is technically not chocolate, as it contains no cocoa solids that give chocolate its flavor. It is often made of cocoa butter, milk and sugar, but can contain hydrogenated fats instead of cocoa butter. North American store brands tend to be somewhat sweeter than European or premium brands.

Unsweetened cocoa powder: I use unsweetened Dutch-process cocoa powder in my baking. It is a dark, rich cocoa powder that has been processed with alkali, which neutralizes its natural acidity. Cocoa powder always needs to be sifted before use because it can be very lumpy, which makes it difficult to incorporate. Use a fine-meshed sieve to remove any lumps before adding cocoa powder to other dry ingredients.

Coffee

Brewed coffee: The recipes in this book were tested using French roast coffee beans, finely ground. To make strong brewed coffee, use a ratio of 2 tbsp (30 mL) finely ground coffee per 6 oz (175 mL) water. This ratio will yield a strong, yet flavorful brewed coffee.

Finely ground coffee: Use a good-quality coffee for your baked goods, as this can greatly affect the taste of your coffee cupcakes. You can either buy whole bean coffee and finely grind the beans yourself in a coffee grinder, or buy the beans already finely ground. I like to use a dark roast coffee in my recipes, such as French, Sumatra or espresso roast.

Instant coffee granules: This is a great way to add coffee flavor without adding brewed coffee. The crystals dissolve instantly in hot liquid.

Dairy

Butter: I recommend using unsalted butter unless otherwise specified in the recipe. The quality is better, the flavor purer, and you can control the saltiness of your recipe. If you are in a pinch and only have salted butter in the house, you can substitute it in most cases in these recipes. Just be sure to omit all other salt called for in the recipe. Margarine cannot automatically be substituted for butter, as it can drastically affect the final product.

Buttermilk: Buttermilk is made from low-fat or nonfat milk that has had a bacterial culture added (somewhat like yogurt), creating a slightly tangy, creamy product. It gives baked goods a delicious flavor and moist texture.

Milk: The recipes in this book were tested using whole milk. Do not substitute nonfat varieties because this can affect the outcome of a recipe.

Cream: Look for whipping (35%) cream or heavy whipping cream. It will keep, refrigerated, for quite a while. For better flavor, look for brands from organic dairies.

Cream cheese: Cream cheese is a fresh cheese made from cow's milk. For quality and consistency, you are better off sticking with name brands.

Sour cream: The addition of sour cream, a high-fat version of buttermilk, helps produce rich and tender results.

Dried fruit

Dried fruit, such as dried cherries, cranberries and apricots, is great to keep on hand for baking.

Eggs

The recipes in this book were tested using large eggs. I generally suggest bringing your eggs to room temperature for baking, but in most of these recipes you can use chilled eggs if need be.

Extracts and flavorings

Always use pure extracts in your baking because they are superior in quality and flavor to artificial flavorings. Imitation vanilla is made from synthetic substances, which imitate only part of the natural vanilla smell and flavor.

Lemon oil: This is a fabulous flavoring that I prefer to lemon extract. It is made from pressed fresh lemons and is 100% pure, with a bright lemon flavor. It is also available in lime and orange. Look for the Boyajian brand (see Sources, page 185).

Flour

All of the recipes in this book were tested using unbleached all-purpose flour, which I feel is a healthier alternative. Bleached flour has been chemically bleached and bromated; I prefer not to use it. You can, however, substitute bleached flour for unbleached flour in these recipes.

Liqueurs

I love to keep a stash of flavored liqueurs and spirits on hand for cooking and baking. Some key ones are rum, orange liqueur or Triple Sec, kirsch (cherry brandy), coffee liqueur and brandy.

Nuts

The recipes in this book use a variety of nuts, such as almonds, walnuts and pecans. Store nuts in the freezer to keep them fresh, as they can go rancid very quickly. *To toast nuts:* Preheat oven to 350°F (180°C). Spread nuts on a foil- or parchment-lined baking sheet and bake for 10 to 12 minutes, stirring occasionally, or until lightly browned and fragrant.

Oil

I like to use canola oil in my recipes, but you can substitute vegetable or soybean oil should you desire. You will want to use a light, flavorless oil, which is why olive oil is not a good choice.

Salt

All of the recipes in this book were tested with plain table salt. Although I like kosher or sea salt on my food, I prefer to use table salt for baking.

Spices

Certain spices are must-haves for desserts, such as ground cinnamon, ground ginger, ground allspice, ground cloves and ground cardamom. Spices tend to go stale quickly, so discard if they are no longer fragrant.

Homemade Marshmallows

Homemade fluffy, sweet marshmallows dusted with confectioner's sugar transport me right back to childhood. Just make sure that you use a powerful stand mixer for this recipe; it won't work with a hand mixer.

Tip

The success of this recipe lies in the mixture being beaten enough; otherwise the marshmallows will be tough.

● **8-inch (20 cm) or 9-inch (23 cm) square pan**

3 tbsp	unflavored gelatin	45 mL
½ cup	water	125 mL

Syrup

2 cups	granulated sugar	500 mL
¾ cup	light corn syrup	175 mL
½ cup	water	125 mL
¼ tsp	salt	1 mL
1 tbsp	vanilla	15 mL

Dusting mixture

1 cup	confectioner's (icing) sugar	250 mL
1 cup	cornstarch	250 mL

1. In the bowl of a stand mixer, combine gelatin and water, stirring just until mixed. Let stand for 30 minutes.

2. *Syrup:* After the gelatin has been sitting for 25 minutes, begin preparing syrup. In a large, heavy-bottomed saucepan, combine sugar, corn syrup, water and salt, stirring until dissolved. Bring to a boil over medium heat. Cover and cook, without stirring, for 3 minutes. Be careful not to let the mixture boil over.

3. Increase heat to high. Uncover and continue cooking, without stirring, until firm-ball stage (248°F/120°C). This will happen very quickly. (Do not overcook the syrup because it will make the marshmallows tough.)

4. Remove from heat and pour syrup slowly over gelatin mixture. Using the wire whisk attachment on the stand mixer, beat mixture on high speed for 15 to 20 minutes or until very thick and fluffy, and mixture increases in volume and climbs up the side of mixer bowl (see Tips, left). When mixture is done, beat in vanilla.

5. *Dusting mixture:* Meanwhile, in a bowl, whisk together confectioner's sugar and cornstarch. Using a small, flat-bottomed metal measuring cup, pack ½ cup (125 mL) of the mixture into pan. Reserve excess cornstarch mixture.

Variation

Beat ½ cup (125 mL) semisweet chocolate chips into the whipped marshmallow mixture at the very end. Spread marshmallow in prepared pan as directed.

6. Scoop marshmallow mixture into prepared pan (this will get a little messy and sticky), smoothing top as best you can. (You can't smooth it completely because it's sticky and thick.) Coat top with some of the reserved cornstarch mixture. Reserve remaining cornstarch mixture. Let marshmallow stand, uncovered, for 12 to 24 hours or until dry and somewhat firm to the touch. (It needs to dry out but not so hard that it can't be cut into pieces.)

7. When marshmallow is dry, invert it onto a cutting board dusted with a little of the reserved cornstarch mixture. Cut marshmallow into squares with kitchen scissors or a knife or into desired shapes with a metal cookie cutter dusted with cornstarch. Dust marshmallow pieces with remaining cornstarch mixture to coat. To store, place marshmallows in an airtight container, dusting well with any remaining cornstarch mixture. Store in cool, dry place for up to 1 week. Before serving marshmallows, lightly shake off extra cornstarch mixture and place on frosted cupcakes. Alternatively, use in Chocolate Surprise Cupcakes (page 22).

Chocolate

Best Chocolate Cupcakes. 18

Chocolate Peanut Butter Cupcakes. 19

Chocolate Gingerbread Cupcakes 20

Chocolate Raspberry Cupcakes. 21

Chocolate Surprise Cupcakes 22

Flourless Chocolate Cupcakes 23

Chocolate Brownie Cupcakes. 24

Orange Chocolate Cupcakes 25

White Chocolate Chip Cupcakes 26

Butterscotch Chocolate Coconut Cupcakes. 27

Very Vanilla Chocolate Chip Cupcakes. 28

Best Chocolate Cupcakes

Makes 12 cupcakes

Here is a great basic chocolate cupcake just asking to be frosted with a creamy, rich topping. I like it topped with everything from Chocolate Fudge Frosting to Cream Cheese Icing (see Frosting suggestions). This recipe is loosely adapted from a recipe in Natalie Haughton's 365 Great Chocolate Desserts.

Tip

These cupcakes freeze well. Wrap them individually in plastic wrap and store them in resealable plastic freezer bags for up to 2 weeks.

Variations

German Chocolate Cupcakes: Omit the chocolate chips in the batter. Frost with Coconut Pecan Frosting (page 154).

Substitute white chocolate chips for the chocolate chips.

- **Preheat oven to 350°F (180°C)**
- **Muffin pan, lined with paper liners**

1¼ cups	all-purpose flour	300 mL
½ cup	unsweetened Dutch-process cocoa powder, sifted	125 mL
¾ tsp	baking soda	3 mL
¼ tsp	salt	1 mL
1 cup	granulated sugar	250 mL
⅓ cup	canola oil	75 mL
1	egg	1
1 tsp	vanilla	5 mL
¾ cup	buttermilk	175 mL
½ cup	semisweet chocolate chips	125 mL
	Frosting (see Frosting suggestions, below)	

1. In a small bowl, whisk together flour, cocoa powder, baking soda and salt.

2. In a large bowl, whisk together sugar, oil, egg and vanilla until smooth. Alternately whisk in flour mixture and buttermilk, making three additions of flour mixture and two of buttermilk, beating until batter is smooth. Stir in chocolate chips.

3. Scoop batter into prepared pan. Bake in preheated oven for 22 to 27 minutes or until tops of cupcakes spring back when lightly touched. Let cool in pan on rack for 10 minutes. Remove from pan and let cool completely on rack. Top cooled cupcakes with frosting.

> **Frosting suggestions:** Chocolate Fudge Frosting (page 149), Cookies and Cream Buttercream (page 157), Vanilla Cream Frosting (page 160) or Cream Cheese Icing (page 158).

Chocolate Peanut Butter Cupcakes

Chocolate and peanut butter are blended together in this recipe to create a fabulously delicious, habit-forming cupcake. I bet you can't eat just one!

Tip

Regular peanut butter, rather than natural-style peanut butter, works best in this recipe.

Variation

Omit the chocolate chips.

- **Preheat oven to 350°F (180°C)**
- **Muffin pan, lined with paper liners**

¾ cup	all-purpose flour	175 mL
¼ cup	unsweetened Dutch-process cocoa powder, sifted	60 mL
1½ tsp	baking powder	7 mL
Pinch	salt	Pinch
½ cup	granulated sugar	125 mL
½ cup	packed brown sugar	125 mL
¼ cup	unsalted butter, at room temperature	60 mL
½ cup	crunchy peanut butter	125 mL
1	egg	1
½ tsp	vanilla	2 mL
⅔ cup	milk	150 mL
½ cup	semisweet chocolate chips	125 mL
	Frosting (see Frosting suggestions, below)	

1. In a small bowl, whisk together flour, cocoa powder, baking powder and salt.

2. In a bowl, using an electric mixer, beat together granulated and brown sugars and butter until well combined. Add peanut butter, beating until smooth. Beat in egg and vanilla until mixture is smooth. Alternately beat in flour mixture and milk, making three additions of flour mixture and two of milk, beating until smooth. Stir in chocolate chips.

3. Scoop batter into prepared pan. Bake in preheated oven for 20 to 25 minutes or until tops of cupcakes spring back when lightly touched. Let cool in pan on rack for 10 minutes. Remove from pan and let cool completely on rack. Top cooled cupcakes with frosting.

> **Frosting suggestions:** Peanut Butter Frosting (page 169), Peanut Butter Fudge Frosting (page 170) or Chocolate Fudge Frosting (page 149).

Chocolate Gingerbread Cupcakes

Gingerbread always makes me think of fall, when I start to crave spiced, hearty foods. Chocolate adds another dimension to gingerbread, which is made even better with some raisins and chocolate chips thrown in for good measure.

Variation

Omit the raisins and substitute 1/3 cup (75 mL) chopped candied ginger.

- **Preheat oven to 350°F (180°C)**
- **Muffin pan, lined with paper liners**

1 1/4 cups	all-purpose flour	300 mL
1/2 cup	unsweetened Dutch-process cocoa powder, sifted	125 mL
2 tsp	ground ginger	10 mL
1 tsp	ground cinnamon	5 mL
3/4 tsp	baking soda	3 mL
1/4 tsp	ground allspice	1 mL
1/4 tsp	salt	1 mL
1 cup	granulated sugar	250 mL
1/3 cup	canola oil	75 mL
1	egg	1
1 tsp	vanilla	5 mL
3/4 cup	buttermilk	175 mL
1/2 cup	semisweet chocolate chips	125 mL
1/3 cup	raisins	75 mL
	Frosting (see Frosting suggestions, below)	

1. In a small bowl, whisk together flour, cocoa powder, ginger, cinnamon, baking soda, allspice and salt.

2. In a large bowl, whisk together sugar, oil, egg and vanilla until smooth. Alternately whisk in flour mixture and buttermilk, making three additions of flour mixture and two of buttermilk, beating until smooth. Stir in chocolate chips and raisins.

3. Scoop batter into prepared pan. Bake in preheated oven for 22 to 27 minutes or until tops of cupcakes spring back when lightly touched. Let cool in pan on rack for 10 minutes. Remove from pan and let cool completely on rack. Top cooled cupcakes with frosting.

> **Frosting suggestions:** Chocolate Fudge Frosting (page 149) or Ginger Cream Cheese Icing (page 161).

Chocolate Raspberry Cupcakes

Chocolate is such a revelation to me. It's a common staple in my house, yet I always find new things to do with it. This recipe is a perfect example. The tangy flavor of raspberries teases the taste buds while the sweet chocolate soothes the palate.

Tip

These cupcakes are best frosted and served the day that they're made.

Variation

Omit raspberries and substitute 1/2 cup (125 mL) peanut butter chips and frost with Peanut Butter Frosting (page 169).

- Preheat oven to 350°F (180°C)
- Muffin pan, lined with paper liners

1 1/2 cups	all-purpose flour	375 mL
1/2 cup	unsweetened Dutch-process cocoa powder, sifted	125 mL
1/2 tsp	baking soda	2 mL
Pinch	salt	Pinch
1 1/4 cups	granulated sugar	300 mL
1/2 cup	canola oil	125 mL
1/2 cup	milk	125 mL
1/2 cup	frozen raspberries, not thawed	125 mL
1 tsp	vanilla	5 mL
2 tbsp	balsamic vinegar	30 mL
	Frosting (see Frosting suggestions, below)	

1. In a small bowl, whisk together flour, cocoa powder, baking soda and salt.

2. In a large bowl, using an electric mixer, beat sugar and oil until well combined. Add milk, frozen raspberries and vanilla, beating just until raspberries are mashed and well incorporated. Add flour mixture, beating until blended. Mix in balsamic vinegar.

3. Scoop batter into prepared pan. Bake in preheated oven for 25 minutes or until tops of cupcakes spring back when lightly touched. Let cool in pan on rack for 10 minutes. Remove from pan and let cool completely on rack. Top cooled cupcakes with frosting.

> **Frosting suggestions:** Chocolate Fudge Frosting (page 149) or Cream Cheese Icing (page 158).

Chocolate Surprise Cupcakes

Makes 12 cupcakes

*My mom called me
the other day to tell
me about a recipe she saw
in Donna Hay Magazine
for a great-looking cupcake
with marshmallow filling.
I didn't have a copy of
the magazine, so I was
inspired to come up with
my own concoction. This
cupcake has been voted a
"10" by friends and family.
Thanks, Mom and Donna!*

Tip

For vegetarians, you
can now find vegetarian
marshmallows in some
specialty health food
stores. To make your
own non-vegetarian
marshmallows (see recipe,
page 15).

- • **Preheat oven to 350°F (180°C)**
- • **Muffin pan, lined with paper liners**

1 cup	all-purpose flour	250 mL
½ tsp	baking powder	2 mL
¼ tsp	each baking soda and salt	1 mL
1 cup	granulated sugar	250 mL
¼ cup	canola oil	60 mL
2	egg whites	2
1 tsp	vanilla	5 mL
2 oz	unsweetened chocolate, melted and cooled slightly	60 g
⅔ cup	buttermilk	150 mL
2 tbsp	chocolate cream liqueur	30 mL
12	large marshmallows (see Tip, left)	12
	Frosting (see suggestions, below)	

1. In a small bowl, whisk together flour, baking powder, baking soda and salt.

2. In a bowl, using an electric mixer, beat together sugar and oil until well combined. Add egg whites, one at a time, beating well after each addition. Beat in vanilla and melted chocolate. Alternately beat in flour mixture and buttermilk, making three additions of flour mixture and two of buttermilk, beating until smooth. Beat in chocolate liqueur.

3. Scoop batter into prepared pan. Bake in preheated oven for 20 to 25 minutes or until tops of cupcakes spring back when lightly touched. Let cool in pan on rack for 5 minutes. Remove cupcakes from pan.

4. While cupcakes are still hot, using a spoon, scoop a hole in the top of each cupcake, scooping down to the center. Push a marshmallow into each hole. Don't worry if the marshmallows stick up a bit from the top of the cupcakes. The warmth of the cupcakes will soften the marshmallows and they will smoosh down. (Discard scooped out cupcake or save to nibble on.) Let cool completely on rack. Top cooled cupcakes with frosting.

> **Frosting suggestions:** Chocolate Fudge Frosting (page 149) or Chocolate Glaze (page 150).

Flourless Chocolate Cupcakes

Makes 12 cupcakes

In my humble opinion, you can't have a cupcake book without including this recipe. These little gems are best served hot, topped with a scoop of ice cream and a sprinkling of cocoa powder. They're a little runny in the center like a molten chocolate cake.

Tips

Make sure to serve these cupcakes immediately, as they are best served hot.

To make almond meal: In a food processor fitted with a metal blade, finely grind about 2/3 cup (150 mL) unsalted whole blanched or unblanched raw almonds. Do not overprocess or you will wind up with almond butter.

Variation

For a less-sweet version, decrease the sugar to 1/2 cup (125 mL).

- **Preheat oven to 350°F (180°C)**
- **Muffin pan, lined with foil liners**

6 oz	bittersweet chocolate, chopped	175 g
2/3 cup	unsalted butter, cut into pieces	150 mL
2	eggs	2
4	egg yolks	4
2/3 cup	granulated sugar	150 mL
2 tbsp	almond meal (see Tips, left)	30 mL
1 tbsp	unsweetened Dutch-process cocoa powder, sifted	15 mL

1. In a microwave-safe bowl, combine chocolate and butter. Microwave, uncovered, on High for 60 to 80 seconds, stirring every 30 seconds, until butter is melted and chocolate is soft. Stir until smooth and chocolate is melted. Set aside and let cool slightly.

2. In a bowl, using an electric mixer, beat eggs, egg yolks and sugar for 2 to 3 minutes or until thick, pale and consistency of soft whipped cream.

3. Fold half of the chocolate mixture into egg mixture. Fold in remaining chocolate mixture. In a small bowl, combine almond meal and cocoa powder. Sift dry ingredients over top of batter and gently fold in until incorporated.

4. Scoop batter into prepared pan and place on baking sheet. Bake in preheated oven for 8 to 12 minutes or until tops of cupcakes are just puffed up. Let cool in pan on rack for 3 minutes. Serve the cupcakes directly in the foil liners placed on individual plates with a spoon for easy scooping.

Chocolate Brownie Cupcakes

Makes 12 cupcakes

How could I have a cupcake book without a brownie-inspired recipe in it? I couldn't, so here's a deliciously chewy and chocolaty cupcake that I am very pleased with. They'll disappear off the cooling rack faster that you can say, "Chocolate brownies."

Tip

These cupcakes are divine served warm with a scoop of ice cream.

Variation

Substitute white chocolate chips for the semisweet.

- **Preheat oven to 325°F (160°C)**
- **Muffin pan, lined with paper liners**

¾ cup	all-purpose flour	175 mL
½ cup	unsweetened Dutch-process cocoa powder, sifted	125 mL
1 tsp	baking powder	5 mL
¼ tsp	salt	1 mL
¾ cup	unsalted butter, melted and cooled slightly	175 mL
⅔ cup	granulated sugar	150 mL
⅔ cup	packed brown sugar	150 mL
½ tsp	vanilla	2 mL
½ tsp	almond extract	2 mL
3	eggs	3
⅔ cup	semisweet chocolate chips	150 mL
	Frosting (see Frosting suggestions, below)	

1. In a small bowl, whisk together flour, cocoa powder, baking powder and salt.

2. In a large bowl, whisk together butter and granulated and brown sugars and butter until smooth. Whisk in vanilla and almond extract. Add eggs, one at a time, beating well after each addition. Add flour mixture, beating until combined. Stir in chocolate chips.

3. Scoop batter into prepared pan. Bake in preheated oven for 28 minutes or until a tester inserted into center comes out with a few crumbs attached and a little melted chocolate. The tops of cupcakes will not spring back when touched. Let cool in pan on rack for 10 minutes. Remove from pan and let cool completely on rack. Top cooled cupcakes with frosting.

> **Frosting suggestions:** Coffee Ice Cream (page 156), Chocolate Fudge Frosting (page 149) or Coffee Buttercream (page 155).

Orange Chocolate Cupcakes

If you love fruit and chocolate together, then you'll love these cupcakes. I like to complement the fruit and chocolate flavor further by topping the cupcakes with Chocolate Fudge Frosting, thereby doubling your pleasure.

Tips

These cupcakes are best frosted and served the day that they're made.

Look for pure orange oil in well-stocked grocery or health food stores. You can also buy it directly from Boyajian (see Sources, page 185). Orange oil tastes like fresh oranges. It's worthwhile seeking out this product.

Variation

You can substitute orange extract for the orange oil in this recipe (although they are not always interchangeable).

- **Preheat oven to 350°F (180°C)**
- **Muffin pan, lined with paper liners**

1 cup	all-purpose flour	250 mL
1 tsp	baking powder	5 mL
1/4 tsp	salt	1 mL
1 cup	granulated sugar	250 mL
1/4 cup	unsalted butter, at room temperature	60 mL
1	egg	1
1 tbsp	grated orange zest	15 mL
1/4 tsp	orange oil (see Tips, left)	1 mL
2/3 cup	milk	150 mL
1/2 cup	semisweet chocolate chips	125 mL
	Frosting (see Frosting suggestions, below)	

1. In a small bowl, whisk together flour, baking powder and salt.

2. In a bowl, using an electric mixer, beat together sugar and butter until well combined. Add egg, beating well. Mix in orange zest and orange oil. Alternately beat in flour mixture and milk, making three additions of flour mixture and two of milk, beating until smooth.

3. Scoop batter into prepared pan. Bake in preheated oven for 20 to 25 minutes or until tops of cupcakes spring back when lightly touched. Let cool in pan on rack for 10 minutes. Remove from pan and let cool completely on rack. Top cooled cupcakes with frosting.

> **Frosting suggestions:** Chocolate Fudge Frosting (page 149) or Orange Cream Cheese Icing (page 168).

White Chocolate Chip Cupcakes

Makes 12 cupcakes

White chocolate is technically not chocolate but it sure tastes divine in vanilla cupcakes. It adds another taste sensation to an otherwise perfect cupcake.

Tip

Look for white chocolate chips in the baking aisle of most supermarkets. If you can't find them, chop a white chocolate bar with a knife to make ½ cup (125 mL).

- **Preheat oven to 350°F (180°C)**
- **Muffin pan, lined with paper liners**

1 cup	all-purpose flour	250 mL
½ tsp	baking powder	2 mL
¼ tsp	baking soda	1 mL
Pinch	salt	Pinch
¾ cup	granulated sugar	175 mL
¼ cup	unsalted butter, at room temperature	60 mL
2	egg whites	2
½ tsp	vanilla	2 mL
⅔ cup	buttermilk	150 mL
½ cup	white chocolate chips or chopped white chocolate (see Tip, left)	125 mL
	Frosting (see Frosting suggestions, below)	

1. In a small bowl, whisk together flour, baking powder, baking soda and salt.

2. In a bowl, using an electric mixer, beat together sugar and butter until well combined. Add egg whites, one at a time, beating well after each addition. Beat in vanilla. Alternately beat in flour mixture and buttermilk, making three additions of flour mixture and two of buttermilk, beating until smooth. Stir in white chocolate chips.

3. Scoop batter into prepared pan. Bake in preheated oven for 20 to 25 minutes or until tops of cupcakes spring back when lightly touched. Let cool in pan on rack for 10 minutes. Remove from pan and let cool completely on rack. Top cooled cupcakes with frosting.

> **Frosting suggestions:** Vanilla Cream Frosting (page 160) or Coffee Buttercream (page 155).

Butterscotch Chocolate Coconut Cupcakes

These are great cupcakes to pack on a picnic. They are a variation on butterscotch brownies, baked in a cupcake shape. You can eat them as is or top them with Chocolate Fudge Frosting.

Tip

Freeze these cupcakes in resealable plastic freezer bags for up to 1 week. Brownies tend to get very dry when stored for too long (even in the freezer).

Variation

Omit the coconut and substitute ½ cup (125 mL) coarsely chopped toasted almonds (see Nuts, page 14).

- **Preheat oven to 350°F (180°C)**
- **Muffin pan, lined with paper liners**

1⅓ cups	all-purpose flour	325 mL
¼ tsp	baking powder	1 mL
¼ tsp	salt	1 mL
½ cup	sweetened flaked coconut	125 mL
¾ cup	packed brown sugar	175 mL
½ cup	unsalted butter, at room temperature	125 mL
1 tsp	vanilla	5 mL
2	eggs	2
⅔ cup	semisweet chocolate chips	150 mL
	Chocolate Fudge Frosting (see recipe, page 149), optional	

1. In a small bowl, whisk together flour, baking powder and salt. Stir in coconut.

2. In a large bowl, using an electric mixer, beat together sugar, butter and vanilla until well combined. Add eggs, one at a time, beating well after each addition. Add flour mixture, beating until smooth. Stir in chocolate chips.

3. Scoop batter into prepared pan. Bake in preheated oven for 25 to 30 minutes or until a tester inserted in center comes out with a few moist crumbs of cupcake and a bit of melted chocolate left on it. Let cool in pan on rack for 10 minutes. Remove from pan and let cool completely on rack. Top cooled cupcakes with frosting, if using.

Very Vanilla Chocolate Chip Cupcakes

Makes 12 cupcakes

I'm sure you know by now how much I love chocolate chips. I couldn't resist putting them in this cupcake, which complements so many different frostings.

Tip

You can find vanilla paste online or in specialty or gourmet markets. If you can't find vanilla paste, you can substitute the same amount of vanilla extract.

- Preheat oven to 350°F (180°C)
- Muffin pan, lined with paper liners

1½ cups	all-purpose flour	375 mL
1 tsp	baking powder	5 mL
¼ tsp	salt	1 mL
1¼ cups	granulated sugar	300 mL
½ cup	unsalted butter, at room temperature	125 mL
3	eggs	3
1 tsp	vanilla paste (see Tip, left)	5 mL
¾ cup	milk	175 mL
½ cup	semisweet chocolate chips	125 mL
	Frosting (see Frosting suggestions, below)	

1. In a small bowl, whisk together flour, baking powder and salt.

2. In a large bowl, using an electric mixer, beat together sugar and butter until well combined. Add eggs, one at a time, beating well after each addition. Beat in vanilla paste. Alternately beat in flour mixture and milk, making three additions of flour mixture and two of milk, beating until smooth. Stir in chocolate chips.

3. Scoop batter into prepared pan. Bake in preheated oven for 23 to 28 minutes or until golden and tops of cupcakes spring back when lightly touched. Let cool in pan on rack for 10 minutes. Remove from pan and let cool completely on rack. Top cooled cupcakes with frosting.

> **Frosting suggestions:** Strawberry Cream Cheese Buttercream (page 172), Orange Cream Cheese Icing (page 168), Easy Buttercream Frosting (page 159) or Chocolate Fudge Frosting (page 149).

Fruit

Apple Crisp Cupcakes 30

Apricot Rum Cupcakes 31

Apricot Spice Cupcakes 32

Blueberry Apricot Cupcakes 33

Cherry Almond Poppy Seed Cupcakes 34

Cranberry Lemon Cupcakes 35

Figgy Cupcakes 36

Mango Coconut Cupcakes 37

Nectarine Cupcakes 38

Orange Date Cupcakes 39

Piña Colada Cupcakes 40

Pineapple Cupcakes 41

Blueberry Rose Cupcakes 42

Tropical Cupcakes 43

Banana Cupcakes. 44

Lemon Yogurt Cupcakes 45

Lemon Buttermilk Cupcakes. 46

Apple Crisp Cupcakes

Makes 12 cupcakes

A mighty chorus of oohs and aahs echoed through our dining room as I served these cupcakes for dessert one evening. They are very moist, with a delicious apple flavor.

Tip

These cupcakes (before frosting) freeze well. Wrap them individually in plastic wrap and store them in resealable plastic freezer bags for up to 2 weeks.

Variation

Substitute 1 pear, peeled, cored and chopped, for the apple.

- **Preheat oven to 350°F (180°C)**
- **Muffin pan, lined with paper liners**

Batter

1 1/2 cups	all-purpose flour	375 mL
1 1/2 tsp	baking powder	7 mL
1/4 tsp	salt	1 mL
1 cup	granulated sugar	250 mL
1/2 cup	unsalted butter, melted and cooled slightly	125 mL
2	eggs	2
1/2 tsp	vanilla	2 mL
1/3 cup	milk	75 mL
1	apple, peeled, cored and diced	1

Streusel

3/4 cup	packed light brown sugar	175 mL
1 tsp	ground cinnamon	5 mL
3 tbsp	unsalted butter, room temperature	45 mL
Pinch	salt	Pinch
	Frosting (see Frosting suggestions, below)	

1. *Batter:* In a bowl, whisk flour, baking powder and salt.

2. In a large bowl, whisk together sugar, butter, eggs and vanilla until smooth. Alternately whisk in flour mixture and milk, making three additions of flour mixture and two of milk, beating until smooth. Stir in apple.

3. *Streusel:* In a bowl, whisk together brown sugar and cinnamon. Add butter and rub in with fingertips until mixture holds together in small, moist clumps.

4. Scoop about half of the batter into prepared pan. Sprinkle streusel over batter. Scoop remaining batter over streusel. Bake in preheated oven for 20 to 25 minutes or until golden brown and tops of cupcakes spring back when lightly touched. Let cool in pan on rack for 10 minutes. Remove from pan and let cool completely on rack. Top cooled cupcakes with frosting.

> **Frosting suggestions:** Cream Cheese Icing (page 158) or Caramel Frosting (page 148).

Apricot Rum Cupcakes

Whether you pronounce apricot with a long a or a short a, your palate will not taste the difference. Additional ingredients, like a healthy splash of rum, make this batter moist and tangy with a hint of the tropics.

Tip

These cupcakes are best frosted and served the day that they're made. If you have to make them ahead of time, leave the cupcakes unwrapped overnight until ready to use. This will prevent them from getting soggy.

Variation

Add ½ cup (125 mL) white chocolate chips to the batter.

• **Preheat oven to 350°F (180°C)**
• **Muffin pan, lined with paper liners**

1 cup	all-purpose flour	250 mL
½ tsp	baking powder	2 mL
¼ tsp	baking soda	1 mL
Pinch	salt	Pinch
⅔ cup	granulated sugar	150 mL
¼ cup	unsalted butter, at room temperature	60 mL
⅓ cup	apricot preserves	75 mL
2	egg whites	2
1 tbsp	dark rum	15 mL
⅔ cup	buttermilk	150 mL
	Frosting (see Frosting suggestions, below)	

1. In a small bowl, whisk together flour, baking powder, baking soda and salt.

2. In a bowl, using an electric mixer, beat together sugar and butter until well combined. Beat in apricot preserves. Add egg whites, one at a time, beating well after each addition. Mix in rum. Alternately beat in flour mixture and buttermilk, making three additions of flour mixture and two of buttermilk, beating until smooth.

3. Scoop batter into prepared pan. Bake in preheated oven for 20 to 25 minutes or until tops of cupcakes spring back when lightly touched. Let cool in pan on rack for 10 minutes. Remove from pan and let cool completely on rack. Top cooled cupcakes with frosting.

> **Frosting suggestions:** Rum Buttercream (page 171) or Vanilla Cream Frosting (page 160).

Apricot Spice Cupcakes

Make this cupcake recipe when apricots are in season. Here, I've given it a sophisticated adult twist (and a little kick) with the addition of allspice and a little ground pepper.

Tip

A mini food processor works very well for puréeing apricots or any soft fruit.

Variation

For an extra zing of apricot flavor, you can add ½ cup (125 mL) diced dried apricots to the batter along with the orange juice.

- **Preheat oven to 350°F (180°C)**
- **Muffin pan, lined with paper liners**

1½ cups	all-purpose flour	375 mL
1 tsp	baking powder	5 mL
1 tsp	ground allspice	5 mL
½ tsp	ground white pepper	2 mL
¼ tsp	salt	1 mL
1¼ cups	granulated sugar	300 mL
½ cup	unsalted butter, at room temperature	125 mL
3	eggs	3
3	ripe apricots, pitted and puréed until smooth	3
⅓ cup	milk	75 mL
⅓ cup	orange juice	75 mL
	Frosting (see Frosting suggestions, below)	

1. In a small bowl, whisk together flour, baking powder, allspice, white pepper and salt.

2. In a large bowl, using an electric mixer, beat together sugar and butter until well combined. Add eggs, one at a time, beating well after each addition until light and fluffy. Add puréed apricots, beating well (it will look curdled, but that's OK). Alternately beat in flour mixture and milk and orange juice, making three additions of flour mixture and one each of milk and orange juice, beating until smooth.

3. Scoop batter into prepared pan. Bake in preheated oven for 23 to 28 minutes or until golden and tops of cupcakes spring back when lightly touched. Let cool in pan on rack for 10 minutes. Remove from pan and let cool completely on rack. Top cooled cupcakes with frosting.

> **Frosting suggestions:** Caramel Frosting (page 148), Ginger Cream Cheese Icing (page 161) or Cream Cheese Icing (page 158).

Best Chocolate Cupcakes (page 18)

Chocolate Surprise Cupcakes (page 22)

Tropical Cupcakes (page 43)

Lemon Yogurt Cupcakes (page 45)

Mocha Cupcakes (page 71)

Candy Bar Cupcakes (page 76)

Ice Cream Cone Cupcakes (page 78)

Peppermint Candy Cupcakes (page 83)

White Cupcakes (page 85)

Chocolate Mint Cupcakes (page 86)

Blueberry Apricot Cupcakes

I call this the all-season cupcake! Make it in summer with fresh fruit and it's outstanding. Make it in winter with frozen fruit, and the flavors remind you of summer. You just can't lose!

Tip

You can find dried apricots in grocery or health food stores.

Variation

Add ½ tsp (2 mL) ground nutmeg to the dry ingredients for a light spice flavor.

- **Preheat oven to 350°F (180°C)**
- **Muffin pan, lined with paper liners**

1½ cups	all-purpose flour	375 mL
1½ tsp	baking powder	7 mL
¼ tsp	salt	1 mL
½ cup	diced dried apricots	125 mL
1 cup	granulated sugar	250 mL
½ cup	unsalted butter, melted and cooled slightly	125 mL
2	eggs	2
⅓ cup	milk	75 mL
1 cup	fresh or frozen blueberries (do not thaw if frozen)	250 mL
	Frosting (see Frosting suggestions, below)	

1. In a small bowl, whisk together flour, baking powder and salt. Stir in diced apricots.

2. In a large bowl, whisk together sugar, butter and eggs until smooth. Alternately whisk in flour mixture and milk, making three additions of flour mixture and two of milk, beating until smooth. Stir in blueberries.

3. Scoop batter into prepared pan. Bake in preheated oven for 20 to 25 minutes or until golden brown and tops of cupcakes spring back when lightly touched. Let cool in pan on rack for 10 minutes. Remove from pan and let cool completely on rack. Top cooled cupcakes with frosting.

> **Frosting suggestions:** Rum Buttercream (page 171), Honey Cream Cheese Frosting (page 162), Vanilla Cream Frosting (page 160) or Easy Buttercream Frosting (page 159).

Cherry Almond Poppy Seed Cupcakes

The almond extract in this recipe brings out the sweet flavor of the cherries, and the poppy seeds add a touch of nutty crunch.

Tip

These cupcakes are best frosted and served the day that they're made.

Variation

Substitute dried cranberries for the cherries.

• **Preheat oven to 350°F (180°C)**
• **Muffin pan, lined with paper liners**

1 cup	all-purpose flour	250 mL
3 tbsp	poppy seeds	45 mL
1/2 tsp	baking powder	2 mL
1/4 tsp	baking soda	1 mL
1/4 tsp	salt	1 mL
1 cup	granulated sugar	250 mL
1/4 cup	canola oil	60 mL
2	egg whites	2
1 tsp	almond extract	5 mL
2/3 cup	buttermilk	150 mL
2/3 cup	dried cherries	150 mL
	Frosting (see Frosting suggestions, below)	

1. In a small bowl, whisk together flour, poppy seeds, baking powder, baking soda and salt.

2. In a bowl, whisk together sugar and oil. Add egg whites, one at a time, beating well after each addition. Beat in almond extract. Alternately whisk in flour mixture and buttermilk, making three additions of flour mixture and two of buttermilk, beating until smooth. Stir in cherries.

3. Scoop batter into prepared pan. Bake in preheated oven for 20 to 25 minutes or until golden brown and tops of cupcakes spring back when lightly touched. Let cool in pan on rack for 10 minutes. Remove from pan and let cool completely on rack. Top cooled cupcakes with frosting.

> **Frosting suggestions:** Whipped Cream Topping (page 175) or Easy Buttercream Frosting (page 159).

Cranberry Lemon Cupcakes

Makes 12 cupcakes

Lemon and cranberry pair well together in this unusual cupcake. Dried cranberries are easily found in bags in well-stocked grocery stores.

Tip

Lemon oil can be found in some specialty food stores or online from Boyajian (see Sources, page 185).

Variation

Substitute dried cherries for the cranberries.

- **Preheat oven to 350°F (180°C)**
- **Muffin pan, lined with paper liners**

1½ cups	all-purpose flour	375 mL
1½ tsp	baking powder	7 mL
¼ tsp	salt	1 mL
1 cup	granulated sugar	250 mL
½ cup	unsalted butter, melted and cooled slightly	125 mL
2	eggs	2
2 tsp	grated lemon zest	10 mL
¼ tsp	lemon oil or lemon extract (see Tip, left)	1 mL
½ cup	milk	125 mL
1 cup	dried cranberries	250 mL
	Frosting (see Frosting suggestions, below)	

1. In a small bowl, whisk together flour, baking powder and salt.

2. In a large bowl, whisk together sugar, butter, eggs, lemon zest and lemon oil until smooth. Alternately whisk in flour mixture and milk, making three additions of flour mixture and two of milk, beating until smooth. Stir in cranberries.

3. Scoop batter into prepared pan. Bake in preheated oven for 20 to 25 minutes or until golden brown and tops of cupcakes spring back when lightly touched. Let cool in pan on rack for 10 minutes. Remove from pan and let cool completely on rack. Top cooled cupcakes with frosting.

> **Frosting suggestions:** Vegan Lemon Glaze (page 181) or Easy Buttercream Frosting (page 159).

Figgy Cupcakes

Fig and orange are a very tasty duo in this cupcake. I have orange and fig trees in my backyard and couldn't resist pairing them up and topping them with a cream cheese icing.

Tip

Either light-color Calimyrna figs or dark-color Mission figs can be used in this recipe.

Variation

Substitute chopped pitted dates for the figs.

- **Preheat oven to 350°F (180°C)**
- **Muffin pan, lined with paper liners**

1½ cups	all-purpose flour	375 mL
1 tsp	baking powder	5 mL
¼ tsp	salt	1 mL
½ cup	coarsely chopped dried figs (see Tip, left)	125 mL
1¼ cups	granulated sugar	300 mL
½ cup	unsalted butter, at room temperature	125 mL
3	eggs	3
1 tsp	vanilla	5 mL
1 tsp	grated orange zest	5 mL
⅓ cup	milk	75 mL
⅓ cup	orange juice	75 mL
	Frosting (see Frosting suggestions, below)	

1. In a small bowl, whisk together flour, baking powder and salt. Stir in chopped figs.

2. In a large bowl, using an electric mixer, beat together sugar and butter until well combined. Add eggs, one at a time, beating well after each addition. Beat in vanilla and orange zest. Alternately beat in flour mixture and milk and orange juice, making three additions of flour mixture and one each of milk and orange juice, beating until smooth.

3. Scoop batter into prepared pan. Bake in preheated oven for 23 to 28 minutes or until golden brown and tops of cupcakes spring back when lightly touched. Let cool in pan on rack for 10 minutes. Remove from pan and let cool completely on rack. Top cooled cupcakes with frosting.

> **Frosting suggestions:** Orange Cream Cheese Icing (page 168) or Ginger Cream Cheese Icing (page 161).

Mango Coconut Cupcakes

Makes 12 cupcakes

My brother, Jon, called me while he was on holiday in Hawaii, insisting that I include a tropical cupcake in the book. I could almost smell the ripe Hawaiian fruit through the telephone and got totally inspired. The mango flavor is deliciously subtle.

Tip

If you can't find fresh ripe mangos, you can usually buy refrigerated mango slices in jars in large supermarkets.

Variation

For a more pronounced mango flavor, increase mango to 1 cup (250 mL) and reduce milk to ¼ cup (60 mL).

- **Preheat oven to 350°F (180°C)**
- **Muffin pan, lined with paper liners**

1½ cups	all-purpose flour	375 mL
½ cup	loosely packed sweetened flaked coconut	125 mL
1½ tsp	baking powder	7 mL
¼ tsp	salt	1 mL
1 cup	granulated sugar	250 mL
½ cup	unsalted butter, melted and cooled slightly	125 mL
2	eggs	2
⅓ cup	milk	75 mL
¾ cup	finely chopped pitted and peeled ripe mango (about 1 mango)	175 mL
	Frosting (see Frosting suggestions, below)	

1. In a small bowl, whisk together flour, coconut, baking powder and salt.

2. In a large bowl, whisk together sugar, butter and eggs until smooth. Alternately whisk in flour mixture and milk, making three additions of flour mixture and two of milk, beating until smooth. Stir in mango.

3. Scoop batter into prepared pan. Bake in preheated oven for 20 to 25 minutes or until golden brown and tops of cupcakes spring back when lightly touched. Let cool in pan on rack for 10 minutes. Remove from pan and let cool completely on rack. Top cooled cupcakes with frosting.

> **Frosting suggestions:** Rum Buttercream (page 171), Cream Cheese Icing (page 158) or Ginger Cream Cheese Icing (page 161).

Nectarine Cupcakes

This delicious cupcake screams "summer"! The secret to this recipe is to find the sweetest-smelling nectarines, which will pump up the fruity flavor tenfold.

Variation

Substitute fresh peach slices for the nectarine slices.

- **Preheat oven to 350°F (180°C)**
- **Muffin pan, lined with paper liners**

1½ cups	all-purpose flour	375 mL
1 tsp	baking powder	5 mL
½ tsp	ground nutmeg	2 mL
¼ tsp	salt	1 mL
1¼ cups	granulated sugar	300 mL
½ cup	unsalted butter, at room temperature	125 mL
3	eggs	3
1 tsp	vanilla	5 mL
2 tsp	grated lemon zest	10 mL
¾ cup	milk	175 mL
2	nectarines, pitted and thinly sliced	2
	Frosting (see Frosting suggestions, below)	

1. In a small bowl, whisk together flour, baking powder, nutmeg and salt.

2. In a large bowl, using an electric mixer, beat together sugar and butter until well combined. Add eggs, one at a time, beating well after each addition until light and fluffy. Add vanilla and lemon zest, beating well. Alternately beat in flour mixture and milk, making three additions of flour mixture and two of milk, beating until smooth. Fold in sliced nectarines.

3. Scoop batter into prepared pan. Bake in preheated oven for 23 to 28 minutes or until golden brown and tops of cupcakes spring back when lightly touched. Let cool in pan on rack for 10 minutes. Remove from pan and let cool completely on rack. Top cooled cupcakes with frosting.

> **Frosting suggestions:** Easy Buttercream Frosting (page 159) or Honey Cream Cheese Frosting (page 162).

Orange Date Cupcakes

I remember my mother baking lots of orange date cakes when I was growing up. I figured that Mom's cake recipe would be a natural in cupcake form.

Tip

These cupcakes are best served the day that they're made.

Variation

Add ⅓ to ½ cup (75 to 125 mL) semisweet chocolate chips to the batter.

- **Preheat oven to 350°F (180°C)**
- **Muffin pan, lined with paper liners**

1 cup	all-purpose flour	250 mL
½ tsp	baking powder	2 mL
¼ tsp	baking soda	1 mL
Pinch	salt	Pinch
¾ cup	chopped pitted dates	175 mL
¾ cup	granulated sugar	175 mL
¼ cup	unsalted butter, at room temperature	60 mL
1 tbsp	grated orange zest	15 mL
2	egg whites	2
½ cup	buttermilk	125 mL
	Frosting (see Frosting suggestions, below)	

1. In a small bowl, whisk together flour, baking powder, baking soda and salt. Stir in dates.

2. In a bowl, using an electric mixer, beat together sugar, butter and orange zest until well combined. Add egg whites, one at a time, beating well after each addition until light and fluffy. Alternately beat in flour mixture and buttermilk, making three additions of flour mixture and two of buttermilk, beating until smooth.

3. Scoop batter into prepared pan. Bake in preheated oven for 20 to 25 minutes or until tops of cupcakes spring back when lightly touched. Let cool in pan on rack for 10 minutes. Remove from pan and let cool completely on rack. Top cooled cupcakes with frosting.

> **Frosting suggestions:** Cream Cheese Icing (page 158), Easy Buttercream Frosting (page 159) or Orange Cream Cheese Icing (page 168).

Piña Colada Cupcakes

You can't have a cupcake book without a piña colada version. My daughter happened to have some friends over one afternoon as I was testing out this recipe, and they went crazy for it. It also had the same effect on adults.

Tip

Use unsweetened canned crushed pineapple that is packed in juice.

Variation

Add ⅓ cup (75 mL) chopped toasted macadamia nuts (see Tip, page 58) to the batter.

- **Preheat oven to 350°F (180°C)**
- **Muffin pan, lined with paper liners**

1 cup	all-purpose flour	250 mL
½ cup	loosely packed sweetened flaked coconut	125 mL
½ tsp	baking powder	2 mL
¼ tsp	baking soda	1 mL
Pinch	salt	Pinch
¾ cup	granulated sugar	175 mL
¼ cup	canola oil	60 mL
1	egg	1
⅓ cup	buttermilk	75 mL
½ cup	crushed pineapple, undrained (see Tip, left)	125 mL
	Frosting (see Frosting suggestions, below)	

1. In a small bowl, whisk together flour, coconut, baking powder, baking soda and salt.

2. In a bowl, whisk together sugar, oil and egg until smooth. Alternately whisk in flour mixture and buttermilk, making three additions of flour mixture and two of buttermilk, beating until smooth. Stir in pineapple.

3. Scoop batter into prepared pan. Bake in preheated oven for 20 to 25 minutes or until tops of cupcakes spring back when lightly touched. Let cool in pan on rack for 10 minutes. Remove from pan and let cool completely on rack. Top cooled cupcakes with frosting.

> **Frosting suggestions:** Rum Buttercream (page 171) or Cream Cheese Icing (page 158).

Pineapple Cupcakes

My husband really enjoys these cupcakes, especially topped with Cream Cheese Icing. He raids the kitchen late at night, unwraps a cupcake and steeps a pot of green or jasmine tea.

Tip

Don't use crushed pineapple in this recipe.

- **Preheat oven to 350°F (180°C)**
- **Muffin pan, lined with paper liners**

1 cup	all-purpose flour	250 mL
1½ tsp	baking powder	7 mL
Pinch	salt	Pinch
¾ cup	granulated sugar	175 mL
⅓ cup	canola oil	75 mL
1	egg	1
½ cup	milk	125 mL
1 cup	drained pineapple chunks, cut in half (see Tip, left)	250 mL
	Frosting (see Frosting suggestions, below)	

1. In a small bowl, whisk together flour, baking powder and salt.

2. In a large bowl, whisk together sugar, oil and egg until smooth. Alternately whisk in flour mixture and milk, making three additions of flour mixture and two of milk, beating until smooth. Stir in pineapple.

3. Scoop batter into prepared pan. Bake in preheated oven for 20 to 25 minutes or until tops of cupcakes spring back when lightly touched. Let cool in pan on rack for 10 minutes. Remove from pan and let cool completely on rack. Top cooled cupcakes with frosting.

> **Frosting suggestions:** Cream Cheese Icing (page 158) or Rum Buttercream (page 171).

Blueberry Rose Cupcakes

Makes 12 cupcakes

The flavoring in this cupcake is a bit unorthodox, but it's delicious nonetheless. The rose flavor is very subtle and pairs nicely with fresh berries and whipped cream.

Tip

Don't use frozen berries for this recipe because they are too soft and wet.

Variation

Instead of using the blueberries in the batter, sprinkle them on top of the whipped cream frosting.

- **Preheat oven to 350°F (180°C)**
- **Muffin pan, lined with paper liners**

1½ cups	all-purpose flour	375 mL
1½ tsp	baking powder	7 mL
¼ tsp	salt	1 mL
1 cup	granulated sugar	250 mL
½ cup	canola oil	125 mL
2	eggs	2
2 tsp	rose water	10 mL
1	drop red food coloring, optional	1
⅓ cup	milk	75 mL
⅔ cup	fresh blueberries or raspberries	150 mL
	Frosting (see Frosting suggestion, below)	

1. In a small bowl, whisk together flour, baking powder and salt.

2. In a large bowl, whisk together sugar, oil and eggs until smooth. Add rose water and red food coloring, if using (only enough to give batter a light pink tint), beating well. Alternately whisk in flour mixture and milk, making three additions of flour mixture and two of milk, beating until smooth. Stir in blueberries.

3. Scoop batter into prepared pan. Bake in preheated oven for 20 to 27 minutes or until golden brown and tops of cupcakes spring back when lightly touched. Let cool in pan on rack for 10 minutes. Remove from pan and let cool completely on rack. Top cooled cupcakes with frosting.

> **Frosting suggestion:** Whipped Cream Topping (page 175), omitting almond syrup and increasing confectioner's (icing) sugar to ⅓ cup (75 mL). Try garnishing the tops of the frosted cupcakes with rose petals (just make sure that they haven't been sprayed with pesticides).

Tropical Cupcakes

Makes 12 cupcakes

I've been fortunate enough to go to Hawaii twice in my life. When I create recipes with a tropical twist, I rely on my fond memories of the sights, sounds, tastes and aromas of the Islands. Maybe, just maybe, if you close your eyes while eating one of these cupcakes, you will be transported there.

Tips

Make sure that the dried fruit is soft before adding it to the batter.

Look for dried pineapple, mango and papaya in bulk and health food stores and in bags at grocery stores in the produce section.

Microwave the dried fruit longer if necessary to soften it.

Variation

Instead of using both dried pineapple and papaya, use only one variety of dried fruit.

- **Preheat oven to 350°F (180°C)**
- **Muffin pan, lined with paper liners**

1/3 cup	finely diced dried pineapple	75 mL
1/3 cup	finely diced dried papaya or mango	75 mL
1/4 cup	coconut rum, divided	60 mL
1 1/2 cups	all-purpose flour	375 mL
1/3 cup	coarsely chopped macadamia nuts, toasted and cooled (see Tip, page 58)	75 mL
3/4 tsp	baking powder	3 mL
1/2 tsp	baking soda	2 mL
1/4 tsp	salt	1 mL
1 1/4 cups	granulated sugar	300 mL
6 tbsp	unsalted butter, room temperature	90 mL
3	egg whites	3
3/4 cup	buttermilk	175 mL
	Frosting (see suggestions, below)	

1. In a microwave-safe bowl, combine pineapple, papaya and 2 tbsp (30 mL) of the coconut rum. Microwave, uncovered, on High for 30 to 60 seconds or until fruit is hot and soft. Cover and let stand until cool. The fruit should absorb most of the rum but not all.

2. In a bowl, whisk together flour, macadamia nuts, baking powder, baking soda and salt.

3. In a large bowl, using an electric mixer, beat together sugar and butter until well combined. Add egg whites, one at a time, beating well after each addition. Alternately beat in flour mixture and buttermilk, making three additions of flour mixture and two of buttermilk, beating until smooth. Stir in soaked fruit and any remaining unabsorbed rum and remaining 2 tbsp (30 mL) coconut rum.

4. Scoop batter into prepared pan. Bake in preheated oven for 20 to 25 minutes or until tops of cupcakes spring back when lightly touched. Let cool in pan on rack for 10 minutes. Remove from pan and let cool on rack. Top cooled cupcakes with frosting.

> **Frosting suggestions:** Rum Buttercream (page 171) or Ginger Cream Cheese Icing (page 161).

Banana Cupcakes

Don't let the simplicity of this recipe fool you. This batter yields a delicate texture that is ready, willing and able to please your taste buds. It's also a fabulous way to use overripe bananas.

Tips

This cupcake (before frosting) freezes well. Wrap them individually in plastic wrap and store them in resealable plastic freezer bags for up to 2 weeks.

Store overripe bananas in the freezer so that when the mood strikes you to bake something with banana (such as this cupcake), you have them at the ready.

Variation

Add ½ cup (125 mL) semisweet chocolate chips to the batter.

- **Preheat oven to 350°F (180°C)**
- **Muffin pan, lined with paper liners**

1¼ cups	all-purpose flour	300 mL
1 tsp	baking soda	5 mL
Pinch	salt	Pinch
1 cup	granulated sugar	250 mL
½ cup	canola oil	125 mL
2	eggs	2
1 cup	mashed banana (about 2 large)	250 mL
1 tsp	vanilla	5 mL
	Frosting (see Frosting suggestions, below)	

1. In a small bowl, whisk together flour, baking soda and salt.

2. In a bowl, whisk together sugar, oil and eggs until smooth. Add banana and vanilla, beating well. Add flour mixture, beating until smooth.

3. Scoop batter into prepared pan. Bake in preheated oven for 24 to 28 minutes or until tops of cupcakes spring back when lightly touched. Let cool in pan on rack for 10 minutes. Remove from pan and let cool completely on rack. Top cooled cupcakes with frosting.

Frosting suggestions: Chocolate Fudge Frosting (page 149), Caramel Frosting (page 148) or Cream Cheese Icing (page 158).

Lemon Yogurt Cupcakes

Makes 12 cupcakes

This cupcake recipe is adapted from Donna Hay's recipe for Lime and Yoghurt Loaf Cake. Let me just say that these cupcakes are to die for! This recipe is a little bit like pound cake with lots of luscious lemon flavor.

Tip

These cupcakes are fabulous when baked in a silicone cupcake pan (see Tools and Equipment, page 11).

Variation

To make lime cupcakes, you can substitute lime juice for the lemon juice, lime zest for the lemon zest, and lime oil for the lemon oil. If you don't have lime oil, just omit it.

- **Preheat oven to 350°F (180°C)**
- **Muffin pan, lined with paper liners**

1¼ cups	all-purpose flour	300 mL
1 tsp	baking powder	5 mL
¼ tsp	salt	1 mL
1 cup	granulated sugar	250 mL
½ cup	unsalted butter, melted and cooled	125 mL
1	egg	1
½ cup	plain yogurt	125 mL
2 tsp	grated lemon zest	10 mL
3 tbsp	freshly squeezed lemon juice	45 mL
½ tsp	lemon oil or lemon extract (see Tip, page 35)	2 mL
	Frosting (see Frosting suggestions, below)	

1. In a small bowl, whisk together flour, baking powder and salt.

2. In a large bowl, whisk together sugar, butter and egg until smooth. Add yogurt, lemon zest and juice, and lemon oil, beating until smooth. Add flour mixture, beating just until smooth.

3. Scoop batter into prepared pan. Bake in preheated oven for 22 to 25 minutes or until tops of cupcakes spring back when lightly touched. Let cool in pan on rack for 10 minutes. Remove from pan and let cool completely on rack. Top cooled cupcakes with frosting.

> **Frosting suggestions:** Vegan Lemon Glaze (page 181), Vanilla Cream Frosting (page 160) or Lemon Cream (page 164).

Lemon Buttermilk Cupcakes

Makes 12 cupcakes

One of my favorite things about living in California is the giant lemon tree in my backyard. I love the puckery citrus taste of lemons and use their juice in almost everything (including these cupcakes). Try slicing these cupcakes in half and filling them with Lemon Curd (page 165) or Vanilla Custard Filling (page 174).

Tip

This recipe tastes much better when made with freshly squeezed lemon juice instead of bottled.

Variation

Add 2 tbsp (30 mL) poppy seeds to the flour mixture.

- **Preheat oven to 350°F (180°C)**
- **Muffin pan, lined with paper liners**

1 cup	all-purpose flour	250 mL
1/2 tsp	baking powder	2 mL
1/4 tsp	baking soda	1 mL
Pinch	salt	Pinch
3/4 cup	granulated sugar	175 mL
1/4 cup	unsalted butter, at room temperature	60 mL
2	egg whites	2
2 tsp	grated lemon zest	10 mL
1/2 tsp	lemon oil or lemon extract (see Tip, page 35)	2 mL
1/3 cup	buttermilk	75 mL
1/4 cup	freshly squeezed lemon juice (see Tip, left)	60 mL
	Frosting (see Frosting suggestions, below)	

1. In a small bowl, whisk together flour, baking powder, baking soda and salt.

2. In a bowl, using an electric mixer, beat together sugar and butter until well combined. Add egg whites, one at a time, beating well after each addition. Add lemon zest and lemon oil, beating well. Alternately beat in flour mixture and buttermilk, making three additions of flour mixture and two of buttermilk, beating until smooth. Add lemon juice, beating just until smooth.

3. Scoop batter into prepared pan and bake in preheated oven for 20 to 25 minutes or until tops of cupcakes spring back when lightly touched. Let cool in pan on rack for 10 minutes. Remove from pan and let cool completely on rack. Top cooled cupcakes with frosting.

> **Frosting suggestions:** Lemon Cream (page 164), Ginger Cream Cheese Icing (page 161) or Easy Buttercream Frosting (page 159).

Nuts

Candied Pecan Cupcakes. 48

Almond Poppy Seed Cupcakes. 49

Awesome Almond Cupcakes 50

Peanut Butter Cupcakes 51

Peanut Butter and Jelly Cupcakes 52

Peanut Butter Chip Cupcakes. 53

Vanilla Peanut Butter Cup Cupcakes. 54

Pistachio Cupcakes 55

Hazelnut Chocolate Cupcakes. 56

White Chocolate Macadamia Cupcakes 58

Candied Pecan Cupcakes

Makes 12 cupcakes

I could eat toasted pecans by the handful right out of the pan. The fragrance and nubbly texture are irresistible. Make extra for munching, because they will inevitably disappear.

Tip

Make sure that your pecans are fresh. I bought some at my local store to test out this recipe and when I opened the bag, they smelled stale. Fresh pecans have a sweet, nutty aroma.

Variation

Stir ½ cup (125 mL) butterscotch baking chips into the batter.

- **Preheat oven to 350°F (180°C)**
- **Baking sheet, lined with foil**
- **Muffin pan, lined with paper liners**

½ cup	chopped pecans (see Tip, left)	125 mL
2 tbsp	packed brown sugar	30 mL
1 cup	all-purpose flour	250 mL
½ tsp	baking powder	2 mL
¼ tsp	baking soda	1 mL
Pinch	salt	Pinch
⅔ cup	packed dark brown sugar	150 mL
¼ cup	unsalted butter, room temperature	60 mL
2	egg whites	2
1 tsp	vanilla	5 mL
⅔ cup	buttermilk	150 mL
	Frosting (see suggestions, below)	

1. In a small nonstick skillet over medium heat, whisk together pecans and 2 tbsp (30 mL) brown sugar. Cook, stirring, until brown sugar is melted and has coated nuts. The pecans should look caramelized and toasted. Remove from heat and spread pecans on prepared baking sheet. Let cool.

2. In a small bowl, whisk together flour, baking powder, baking soda and salt.

3. In a bowl, using an electric mixer, beat together ⅔ cup (150 mL) dark brown sugar and butter until well combined. Add egg whites, one at a time, beating well after each addition. Mix in vanilla and caramelized pecans. Alternately beat in flour mixture and buttermilk, making three additions of flour mixture and two of buttermilk, beating until smooth.

4. Scoop batter into prepared pan. Bake in preheated oven for 20 to 25 minutes or until tops of cupcakes spring back when lightly touched. Let cool in pan on rack for 10 minutes. Remove from pan and let cool completely on rack. Top cooled cupcakes with frosting.

Frosting suggestions: Caramel Frosting (page 148), Maple Buttercream (page 167) or Coconut Pecan Frosting (page 154).

Almond Poppy Seed Cupcakes

I made these cupcakes for my brother's 33rd birthday party, and they were received with great accolades. Everyone loved them, especially heaped with a mound of frosting. There's nothing like watching adults turn into children.

Tip

These cupcakes are best frosted and served the day that they're made.

Variation

Omit the sliced almonds and use ½ cup (125 mL) dried cherries instead.

- Preheat oven to 350°F (180°C)
- Muffin pan, lined with paper liners

1 cup	all-purpose flour	250 mL
2 tbsp	poppy seeds	30 mL
½ tsp	baking powder	2 mL
¼ tsp	baking soda	1 mL
¼ tsp	salt	1 mL
¾ cup	granulated sugar	175 mL
¼ cup	unsalted butter, at room temperature	60 mL
2	egg whites	2
1 tsp	almond extract	5 mL
⅔ cup	buttermilk	150 mL
⅓ cup	sliced almonds	75 mL
	Frosting (see Frosting suggestions, below)	

1. In a small bowl, whisk together flour, poppy seeds, baking powder, baking soda and salt.

2. In a bowl, using an electric mixer, beat together sugar and butter until well combined. Add egg whites, one at a time, beating well after each addition. Beat in almond extract. Alternately beat in flour mixture and buttermilk, making three additions of flour mixture and two of buttermilk, beating until smooth. Beat in almonds.

3. Scoop batter into prepared pan. Bake in preheated oven for 20 to 25 minutes or until tops of cupcakes spring back when lightly touched. Let cool in pan on rack for 10 minutes. Remove from pan and let cool completely on rack. Top cooled cupcakes with frosting.

> **Frosting suggestions:** Cream Cheese Icing (page 158), Chocolate Fudge Frosting (page 149) or Orange Cream Cheese Icing (page 168).

Awesome Almond Cupcakes

I love anything almond and everything with almond flavor. These cupcakes pack a triple-almond punch.

Tips

For a stronger almond flavor, add an additional 1/2 tsp (2 mL) almond extract.

You can usually find almond-flavored syrup in the coffee aisle of large supermarkets or at specialty coffeehouses.

Variation

Add 1/2 cup (125 mL) semisweet chocolate chips for a chocolaty version.

- **Preheat oven to 350°F (180°C)**
- **Muffin pan, lined with paper liners**

1 1/4 cups	all-purpose flour	300 mL
1/3 cup	almond meal (see Tips, page 23)	75 mL
1 1/2 tsp	baking powder	7 mL
1/4 tsp	salt	1 mL
3/4 cup	granulated sugar	175 mL
1/2 cup	canola oil	125 mL
2	eggs	2
1/2 tsp	almond extract	2 mL
1/3 cup	milk	75 mL
1/4 cup	almond-flavored syrup (see Tips, left)	60 mL
	Frosting (see Frosting suggestions, below)	

1. In a small bowl, whisk together flour, almond meal, baking powder and salt.

2. In a large bowl, whisk together sugar, oil, eggs and almond extract until smooth. Alternately beat in flour mixture and milk, making three additions of flour mixture and two of milk, beating until smooth. Mix in almond-flavored syrup.

3. Scoop batter into prepared pan. Bake in preheated oven for 20 to 25 minutes or until golden brown and tops of cupcakes spring back when lightly touched. Let cool in pan on rack for 10 minutes. Remove from pan and let cool completely on rack. Top cooled cupcakes with frosting.

> **Frosting suggestions:** Whipped Cream Topping (page 175), Chocolate Fudge Frosting (page 149) or Easy Buttercream Frosting (page 159).

Peanut Butter Cupcakes

Makes 12 cupcakes

How many different ways can you make peanut butter cupcakes? Lots, and here's proof, because this is yet another version for die-hard peanut butter lovers.

Tip

Regular peanut butter makes a smoother batter than natural-style peanut butter, so use it in this recipe.

Variation

Stick a piece (or square) of semisweet chocolate into the center of each unbaked cupcake.

- **Preheat oven to 350°F (180°C)**
- **Muffin pan, lined with paper liners**

1 cup	all-purpose flour	250 mL
1½ tsp	baking powder	7 mL
Pinch	salt	Pinch
½ cup	granulated sugar	125 mL
½ cup	packed brown sugar	125 mL
¼ cup	unsalted butter, at room temperature	60 mL
½ cup	crunchy peanut butter	125 mL
1	egg	1
½ tsp	vanilla	2 mL
⅔ cup	milk	150 mL
	Frosting (see Frosting suggestions, below)	

1. In a small bowl, whisk together flour, baking powder and salt.

2. In a large bowl, using an electric mixer, beat together granulated and brown sugars and butter until well combined. Add peanut butter, beating until smooth. Add egg and vanilla, beating well. Alternately beat in flour mixture and milk, making three additions of flour mixture and two of milk, beating until smooth.

3. Scoop batter into prepared pan. Bake in preheated oven for 20 to 25 minutes or until tops of cupcakes spring back when lightly touched. Let cool in pan on rack for 10 minutes. Remove from pan and let cool completely on rack. Top cooled cupcakes with frosting.

> **Frosting suggestions:** Peanut Butter Frosting (page 169) or Peanut Butter Fudge Frosting (page 170).

Peanut Butter and Jelly Cupcakes

Children flip for this cupcake because most kids love peanut butter and jelly. I fill these divine cupcakes with strawberry jam, but you can get creative and fill them with whatever jam or jelly you choose. You can even follow in the New England tradition and fill them instead with Marshmallow Fluff or marshmallow crème.

Tip

I would definitely plan on making and frosting these cupcakes the day that you're planning to serve them.

Variation

Grape, cherry or other berry jams are particularly tasty.

- **Preheat oven to 350°F (180°C)**
- **Muffin pan, lined with paper liners**

1 cup	all-purpose flour	250 mL
1/2 tsp	baking powder	2 mL
1/4 tsp	baking soda	1 mL
Pinch	salt	Pinch
3/4 cup	granulated sugar	175 mL
1/4 cup	unsalted butter, at room temperature	60 mL
2	egg whites	2
1 tsp	vanilla	5 mL
2/3 cup	buttermilk	150 mL
1/3 cup	strawberry jam	75 mL
	Peanut Butter Frosting (see recipe, page 169)	

1. In a small bowl, whisk together flour, baking powder, baking soda and salt.

2. In a bowl, using an electric mixer, beat together sugar and butter until well combined. Add egg whites, one at a time, beating well after each addition. Beat in vanilla. Alternately beat in flour mixture and buttermilk, making three additions of flour mixture and two of buttermilk, beating until smooth.

3. Scoop batter into prepared pan. Bake in preheated oven for 20 to 25 minutes or until tops of cupcakes spring back when lightly touched. Let cool in pan on rack for 10 minutes. Remove from pan and let cool completely on rack.

4. Remove paper liners from cupcakes. Slice cupcakes in half horizontally. Spread bottoms with jam, replacing tops. Let set for 10 minutes. Top filled cupcakes with Peanut Butter Frosting.

Peanut Butter Chip Cupcakes

Makes 12 cupcakes

Wow, a vanilla cupcake with peanut butter chips and a fluffy topping of Peanut Butter Frosting (or Chocolate Fudge Frosting) is nothing short of divine!

Tip

If you can't find peanut butter chips in your local grocery store, you can substitute another baking chip of your choice.

Variation

You can omit the peanut butter chips for a great basic vanilla cupcake.

- **Preheat oven to 350°F (180°C)**
- **Muffin pan, lined with paper liners**

1 1/4 cups	all-purpose flour	300 mL
1 tsp	baking powder	5 mL
1/4 tsp	salt	1 mL
1 cup	granulated sugar	250 mL
1/2 cup	unsalted butter, at room temperature	125 mL
2	eggs	2
1 tsp	vanilla	5 mL
1/2 cup	milk	125 mL
1/2 cup	peanut butter chips	125 mL
	Frosting (see Frosting suggestions, below)	

1. In a small bowl, whisk together flour, baking powder and salt.

2. In a large bowl, using an electric mixer, beat together sugar and butter until well combined. Add eggs, one at a time, beating well after each addition. Beat in vanilla. Alternately beat in flour mixture and milk, making three additions of flour mixture and two of milk, beating until smooth. Stir in peanut butter chips.

3. Scoop batter into prepared pan. Bake in preheated oven for 20 to 25 minutes or until tops of cupcakes spring back when lightly touched. Let cool in pan on rack for 10 minutes. Remove from pan and let cool completely on rack. Top cooled cupcakes with frosting.

> **Frosting suggestions:** Peanut Butter Frosting (page 169), Chocolate Fudge Frosting (page 149) or Easy Buttercream Frosting (page 159).

Vanilla Peanut Butter Cup Cupcakes

Makes 12 cupcakes

These cupcakes were a huge hit at my sister-in-law Randie's house. Everyone flipped for them! "There goes my Atkins/Weight Watchers/ Hollywood low-carb diet," said the crowd. Now that's a cupcake!

Tip

I like to keep chocolate peanut butter cup candies on hand so that I can throw these cupcakes together whenever the mood strikes me.

Variation

Substitute ½ to ⅔ cup (125 to 150 mL) candy-coated chocolate peanut butter candies, such as Reese's Pieces, for the chocolate peanut butter cup candies.

- • Preheat oven to 350°F (180°C)
- • Muffin pan, lined with paper liners

1 cup	all-purpose flour	250 mL
½ tsp	baking powder	2 mL
¼ tsp	baking soda	1 mL
¼ tsp	salt	1 mL
1 cup	granulated sugar	250 mL
¼ cup	canola oil	60 mL
2	egg whites	2
1 tsp	vanilla	5 mL
⅔ cup	buttermilk	150 mL
8	milk chocolate peanut butter cup candies, coarsely chopped	8
	Frosting (see Frosting suggestions, below)	

1. In a small bowl, whisk together flour, baking powder, baking soda and salt.

2. In a bowl, whisk together sugar and oil. Add egg whites, one at a time, beating well after each addition. Beat in vanilla. Alternately beat in flour mixture and buttermilk, making three additions of flour mixture and two of buttermilk, beating until smooth. Mix in peanut butter candies, being careful not to mash them.

3. Scoop batter into prepared pan. Bake in preheated oven for 20 to 25 minutes or until tops of cupcakes spring back when lightly touched. Let cool in pan on rack for 10 minutes. Remove from pan and let cool completely on rack. Top cooled cupcakes with frosting.

> **Frosting suggestions:** Peanut Butter Frosting (page 169) or Chocolate Fudge Frosting (page 149).

Pistachio Cupcakes

Makes 12 cupcakes

I think pistachios are a delicious snack right out of hand. They're even better when ground up and added to baked goods, such as these cupcakes.

Tips

Use natural shelled pistachios for this recipe, not the ones that are dyed red in their shells.

Use a food processor to finely grind the nuts. Be careful not to overprocess the nuts or else they will turn into nut butter.

Variation

Serve these cupcakes warm with a drizzle of Hot Fudge Sauce (page 163) instead of the frosting.

- **Preheat oven to 350°F (180°C)**
- **Muffin pan, lined with paper liners**

1¼ cups	all-purpose flour	300 mL
½ cup	pistachios, finely ground	125 mL
1 tsp	baking powder	5 mL
¼ tsp	salt	1 mL
1 cup	granulated sugar	250 mL
½ cup	unsalted butter, at room temperature	125 mL
3	eggs	3
½ tsp	almond extract	2 mL
¾ cup	milk	175 mL
	Frosting (see Frosting suggestions, below)	

1. In a small bowl, whisk together flour, pistachios, baking powder and salt.

2. In a large bowl, using an electric mixer, beat together sugar and butter until well combined. Add eggs, one at a time, beating well after each addition. Beat in almond extract. Alternately beat in flour mixture and milk, making three additions of flour mixture and two of milk, beating until smooth.

3. Scoop batter into prepared pan. Bake in preheated oven for 24 to 28 minutes or until golden brown and tops of cupcakes spring back when lightly touched. Let cool in pan on rack for 10 minutes. Remove from pan and let cool completely on rack. Top cooled cupcakes with frosting.

> **Frosting suggestions:** Easy Buttercream Frosting (page 159) or Cream Cheese Icing (page 158).

Hazelnut Chocolate Cupcakes

Makes 18 cupcakes

When I was a teenager, my mother returned from a trip to Europe with a jar of the most delicious chocolate hazelnut spread this sweet-crazed teenager had ever tasted. So if you love chocolate and hazelnuts as much as I do, then this cupcake is for you.

Tip

To make hazelnut meal: Place ½ cup (125 mL) hazelnuts in a single layer on a foil- or parchment-lined baking sheet. Bake in center of preheated 350°F (180°C) oven for 10 minutes or until lightly browned and skins are slightly blistered. Wrap nuts in a clean dry kitchen towel and let stand for 1 minute. Rub nuts in towel to remove loose skins (it's OK if you can't remove all of the skins). Let cool completely. In a food processor fitted with a metal blade, finely grind nuts. Do not overprocess or you will wind up with hazelnut butter. It will be powdery with slightly bigger bits of nuts in it, which is OK.

- Preheat oven to 350°F (180°C)
- **2 muffin pans (one 12-cup and one 6-cup), lined with paper liners**

1¼ cups	all-purpose flour	300 mL
½ cup	hazelnut meal (see Tip, left)	125 mL
1 tsp	baking powder	5 mL
¼ tsp	salt	1 mL
1 cup	semisweet chocolate chips, finely chopped (see Tip, right)	250 mL
1¼ cups	granulated sugar	300 mL
½ cup	unsalted butter, at room temperature	125 mL
3	eggs	3
1 tsp	vanilla	5 mL
¾ cup	milk	175 mL
	Frosting (see Frosting suggestions, right)	

1. In a small bowl, whisk together flour, hazelnut meal, baking powder and salt. Stir in chopped chocolate chips.

2. In a large bowl, using an electric mixer, beat together sugar and butter until well combined. Add eggs, one at a time, beating well after each addition. Beat in vanilla. Alternately beat in flour mixture and milk, making three additions of flour mixture and two of milk, beating until smooth.

Tip

A great way to chop the chocolate chips is in a food processor (especially a mini food processor).

3. Scoop batter into prepared pans. Bake in preheated oven for 20 to 25 minutes or until golden brown and tops of cupcakes spring back when lightly touched. Let cool in pans on rack for 10 minutes. Remove from pans and let cool completely on rack. Top cooled cupcakes with frosting.

Frosting suggestions: Chocolate Hazelnut Frosting (page 152) or Chocolate Fudge Frosting (page 149).

White Chocolate Macadamia Cupcakes

White chocolate and macadamia nuts — just think of the possibilities. Whenever I pair these ingredients together, I imagine them as the dynamic duo: always pleasing, always.

Tip

I like to toast the macadamia nuts in a dry nonstick skillet over medium heat, stirring constantly, for about 5 minutes.

Variation

Substitute semisweet chocolate chips for the white chocolate chips and almonds for the macadamia nuts.

- **Preheat oven to 350°F (180°C)**
- **Muffin pan, lined with paper liners**

1½ cups	all-purpose flour	375 mL
¾ cup	macadamia nuts, coarsely chopped, toasted and cooled (see Tip, left)	175 mL
1½ tsp	baking powder	7 mL
¼ tsp	salt	1 mL
1 cup	granulated sugar	250 mL
½ cup	canola oil	125 mL
2	eggs	2
⅓ cup	milk	75 mL
½ cup	white chocolate chips	125 mL
	Cream Cheese Icing (see recipe, page 158)	
¼ cup	toasted macadamia nuts for garnish	60 mL

1. In a small bowl, whisk together flour, macadamia nuts, baking powder and salt.

2. In a large bowl, whisk together sugar, oil and eggs until smooth. Alternately beat in flour mixture and milk, making three additions of flour mixture and two of milk, beating just until smooth. Stir in white chocolate chips.

3. Scoop batter into prepared pan. Bake in preheated oven for 22 to 26 minutes or until golden brown and tops of cupcakes spring back when lightly touched. Let cool in pan on rack for 10 minutes. Remove from pan and let cool completely on rack. Top cooled cupcakes with Cream Cheese Icing and garnish with macadamia nuts.

Adults Only

Pimm's Cupcakes 60

Crème de Menthe Cupcakes 61

Cassis Cupcakes 62

Kahlúa Cupcakes 63

Margarita Cupcakes 64

Sherry Apricot Cupcakes 66

Rum Raisin Cupcakes 67

Malted Espresso Cupcakes 68

Cappuccino Cupcakes 69

Jay's Favorite Chocolate Cupcakes 70

Mocha Cupcakes 71

Espresso Dark Brownie Cupcakes 72

Earl Grey Cupcakes 73

Green Tea Cupcakes 74

Pimm's Cupcakes

Pimm's Cup is a famous summertime drink in Great Britain that's deliciously refreshing on a hot day. I thought it would be fun to turn this drink into a cupcake. Cheerio!

Tips

You should be able to find Pimm's No. 1 liqueur in liquor stores and supermarkets where liquor is sold.

You can find lemon oil in some gourmet specialty stores or online from Boyajian (see Sources, page 185).

- **Preheat oven to 350°F (180°C)**
- **Muffin pan, lined with paper liners**

1½ cups	all-purpose flour	375 mL
1½ tsp	baking powder	7 mL
¼ tsp	salt	1 mL
1 cup	granulated sugar	250 mL
½ cup	canola oil	125 mL
2	eggs	2
2 tsp	grated lemon zest	10 mL
½ tsp	lemon oil or lemon extract (see Tips, left)	2 mL
⅓ cup	milk	75 mL
⅓ cup	Pimm's No. 1 liqueur	75 mL

Topping

¼ cup	Pimm's No. 1 liqueur	60 mL
	Frosting (see Frosting suggestions, below)	

1. In a small bowl, whisk together flour, baking powder and salt.

2. In a large bowl, whisk together sugar, oil and eggs until smooth. Add lemon zest and lemon oil. Alternately whisk in flour mixture and milk and Pimm's liqueur, making three additions of flour mixture and one each of milk and liqueur, beating just until smooth.

3. Scoop batter into prepared pan. Bake in preheated oven for 20 to 25 minutes or until golden brown and tops of cupcakes spring back when lightly touched. Let cool in pan on a rack for 10 minutes.

4. *Topping:* Using a skewer, poke four or five holes in top of each cupcake. Drizzle 1 tsp (5 mL) Pimm's liqueur over top of each cupcake. Transfer to rack and let cool completely. Top cooled cupcakes with frosting.

> **Frosting suggestions:** Lemon Cream (page 164), Vegan Lemon Glaze (page 181) or Easy Buttercream Frosting (page 159).

Crème de Menthe Cupcakes

Here is a cupcake you will never forget because of its green color. It's ideal for St. Patrick's Day or any occasion for which you need a minty cupcake. It tastes like mint chocolate chip ice cream, without the chill.

Tip

You can find crème de menthe at most liquor stores.

Variation

For a non-chocolate version, omit the chocolate chips.

• **Preheat oven to 350°F (180°C)**
• **Muffin pan, lined with paper liners**

1½ cups	all-purpose flour	375 mL
1½ tsp	baking powder	7 mL
¼ tsp	salt	1 mL
1 cup	granulated sugar	250 mL
½ cup	unsalted butter, melted and cooled slightly	125 mL
2	eggs	2
⅓ cup	milk	75 mL
⅓ cup	crème de menthe	75 mL
½ cup	semisweet chocolate chips	125 mL
	Frosting (see Frosting suggestions, below)	

1. In a small bowl, whisk together flour, baking powder and salt.

2. In a large bowl, whisk together sugar, butter and eggs until smooth. Alternately whisk in flour mixture and milk and crème de menthe, making three additions of flour mixture and one each of milk and crème de menthe, beating until smooth. Mix in chocolate chips.

3. Scoop batter into prepared pan. Bake in preheated oven for 20 to 25 minutes or until golden brown and tops of cupcakes spring back when lightly touched. Let cool in pan on rack for 10 minutes. Remove from pan and let cool completely on rack. Top cooled cupcakes with frosting.

> **Frosting suggestions:** Chocolate Fudge Frosting (page 149) or Chocolate Glaze (page 150).

Cassis Cupcakes

This cupcake is a fun flavor twist on the whole cupcake theme. The subtle taste of crème de cassis, the French black currant liqueur, is divine. Not only does it taste great, but your kitchen will be filled with the wafting aroma of heavenly baking.

Tip

You can find crème de cassis at liquor stores.

Variation

Add a drop of red food coloring to the batter to give it a light pink hue.

- **Preheat oven to 350°F (180°C)**
- **Muffin pan, lined with paper liners**

1½ cups	all-purpose flour	375 mL
1½ tsp	baking powder	7 mL
¼ tsp	salt	1 mL
1 cup	granulated sugar	250 mL
½ cup	canola oil	125 mL
2	eggs	2
¼ cup	milk	60 mL
½ cup	crème de cassis	125 mL
	Easy Buttercream Frosting (see recipe, page 159)	

1. In a small bowl, whisk together flour, baking powder and salt.

2. In a large bowl, whisk together sugar, oil and eggs until smooth. Alternately whisk in flour mixture and milk and crème de cassis, making three additions of flour mixture and one each of milk and liqueur, beating until smooth.

3. Scoop batter into prepared pan. Bake in preheated oven for 20 to 25 minutes or until golden brown and tops of cupcakes spring back when lightly touched. Remove from pan and let cool completely on rack. Top cooled cupcakes with Easy Buttercream Frosting.

Kahlúa Cupcakes

In my opinion, Kahlúa makes an outstanding addition to cupcakes. It's definitely an adult cupcake, but, hey, sometimes we need to have our own treats.

Tip

These cupcakes are best frosted and served the day that they're made.

Variation

Fill these cupcakes with Chocolate Mousse Filling (page 151).

- Preheat oven to 350°F (180°C)
- Muffin pan, lined with paper liners

1 cup	all-purpose flour	250 mL
1/2 tsp	baking powder	2 mL
1/4 tsp	baking soda	1 mL
Pinch	salt	Pinch
1/3 cup	Kahlúa or coffee-flavored liqueur	75 mL
2 tsp	instant coffee granules	10 mL
3/4 cup	granulated sugar	175 mL
1/3 cup	unsalted butter, at room temperature	75 mL
2	egg whites	2
1/3 cup	buttermilk	75 mL
	Frosting (see Frosting suggestions, below)	

1. In a small bowl, whisk together flour, baking powder, baking soda and salt.

2. In a small bowl, whisk together Kahlúa and instant coffee.

3. In a bowl, using an electric mixer, beat together sugar and butter until well combined. Add egg whites, one at a time, beating well after each addition. Alternately beat in flour mixture and buttermilk and liqueur mixture, making three additions of flour mixture and one each of buttermilk and liqueur mixture, beating until smooth.

4. Scoop batter into prepared pan. Bake in preheated oven for 20 to 25 minutes or until tops of cupcakes spring back when lightly touched. Let cool in pan on rack for 10 minutes. Remove from pan and let cool completely on rack. Top cooled cupcakes with frosting.

> **Frosting suggestions:** Coffee Buttercream (page 155) or Chocolate Fudge Frosting (page 149).

Margarita Cupcakes

Makes 12 cupcakes

What better defines a summer afternoon than a margarita? Imagine all of the delicious flavors of your favorite drink rolled into a miniature cake. This cupcake is tops!

Tips

These cupcakes are best eaten when they're freshly baked.

You can order lime oil online from Boyajian (see Sources, page 185) or buy it in specialty food or gourmet stores.

Superfine, or baker's, sugar is ultrafine granulated sugar, which dissolves very quickly in liquid. If you can't find it in your local grocery store, you can make your own: process granulated sugar in a food processor until very finely ground.

- **Preheat oven to 350°F (180°C)**
- **Muffin pan, lined with paper liners**

1½ cups	all-purpose flour	375 mL
1½ tsp	baking powder	7 mL
¼ tsp	salt	1 mL
¼ cup	freshly squeezed lime juice	60 mL
2 tbsp	orange-flavored liqueur, such as Triple Sec	30 mL
1 cup	granulated sugar	250 mL
½ cup	canola oil	125 mL
2	eggs	2
½ tsp	lime oil or grated lime zest (see Tips, left)	2 mL
⅓ cup	milk	75 mL
Syrup		
3 tbsp	light corn syrup	45 mL
2 tbsp	superfine sugar (see Tips, left)	30 mL
1 tbsp	tequila	15 mL
1 tbsp	freshly squeezed lime juice	15 mL
	Frosting (see Frosting suggestions, right)	

1. In a small bowl, whisk together flour, baking powder and salt.

2. In a small bowl, whisk together lime juice and liqueur.

3. In a large bowl, whisk together sugar, oil, eggs and lime oil until smooth. Alternately whisk in flour mixture and milk and liqueur mixture, making three additions of flour mixture and one each of milk and liqueur mixture, beating just until smooth.

4. Scoop batter into prepared pan. Bake in preheated oven for 20 to 25 minutes or until golden brown and tops of cupcakes spring back when lightly touched. Let cool in pan on a rack for just 5 minutes.

5. *Syrup:* Using a skewer, poke four or five holes in top of each warm cupcake. In a small bowl, whisk together corn syrup, sugar, tequila and lime juice. Drizzle syrup over top of each cupcake. Let cool in pan on rack for 10 minutes. Remove from pan and let cool completely on rack. Top cooled cupcakes with frosting.

> **Frosting suggestions:** Easy Buttercream Frosting (page 159), or Whipped Cream Topping (page 175), omitting almond syrup and increasing sugar to $\frac{1}{3}$ cup (75 mL).

Sherry Apricot Cupcakes

The flavor of sherry combined with apricots is, quite simply, outstanding! My mother thought that this cupcake was great, and the flavor spoke for itself, even unfrosted.

Tip

Three easy ways to chop dried apricots are with a chef's knife, a pair of kitchen scissors or in a food processor.

Variation

Substitute whole golden raisins for the chopped apricots.

- **Preheat oven to 350°F (180°C)**
- **Muffin pan, lined with paper liners**

1 cup	all-purpose flour	250 mL
½ tsp	baking powder	2 mL
¼ tsp	baking soda	1 mL
Pinch	salt	Pinch
¾ cup	granulated sugar	175 mL
¼ cup	unsalted butter, at room temperature	60 mL
2	egg whites	2
½ cup	buttermilk	125 mL
½ cup	dried apricots, finely chopped	125 mL
3 tbsp	cream sherry	45 mL
	Frosting (see Frosting suggestions, below)	

1. In a small bowl, whisk together flour, baking powder, baking soda and salt.

2. In a bowl, using an electric mixer, beat together sugar and butter until well combined. Add egg whites, one at a time, beating well after each addition. Alternately beat in flour mixture and buttermilk, making three additions of flour mixture and two of buttermilk, beating until smooth. Mix in dried apricots and sherry.

3. Scoop batter into prepared pan. Bake in preheated oven for 20 to 25 minutes or until tops of cupcakes spring back when lightly touched. Let cool in pan on rack for 10 minutes. Remove from pan and let cool completely on rack. Top cooled cupcakes with frosting.

> **Frosting suggestions:** Caramel Frosting (page 148) or Rum Buttercream (page 171), substituting sherry for the rum.

Rum Raisin Cupcakes

Makes 12 cupcakes

This adult cupcake has the sharp, spicy taste of dark rum, which contrasts nicely with the sweet flavor of the frosting. This cupcake is a definite hit with raisin lovers.

Tip

These cupcakes are best served the day that they're made.

Variation

Substitute dried cherries for the raisins.

- **Preheat oven to 350°F (180°C)**
- **Muffin pan, lined with paper liners**

½ cup	raisins	125 mL
¼ cup	dark rum	60 mL
1½ cups	all-purpose flour	375 mL
1½ tsp	baking powder	7 mL
¼ tsp	salt	1 mL
1 cup	granulated sugar	250 mL
½ cup	canola oil	125 mL
2	eggs	2
⅓ cup	milk	75 mL

Topping

¼ cup	dark rum	60 mL
	Frosting (see Frosting suggestions, below)	

1. In a microwave-safe bowl or cup, combine raisins and rum. Microwave, uncovered, on High for 30 to 60 seconds or until raisins are hot and soft. Let cool to room temperature.

2. In a small bowl, whisk together flour, baking powder and salt.

3. In a large bowl, whisk together sugar, oil and eggs until smooth. Alternately whisk in flour mixture and milk, making three additions of flour mixture and two of milk, beating until smooth. Mix in cooled raisin mixture and any remaining rum from dish.

4. Scoop batter into prepared pan. Bake in preheated oven for 20 to 25 minutes or until golden brown and tops of cupcakes spring back when lightly touched. Let cool in pan on a rack for just 5 minutes.

5. *Topping:* Using a skewer, poke four or five holes in top of each warm cupcake. Drizzle 1 tsp (5 mL) dark rum over top of each cupcake. Let cool in pan on rack for 10 minutes. Remove from pan and let cool completely on rack. Top cooled cupcakes with frosting.

> **Frosting suggestions:** Rum Buttercream (page 171) or Caramel Frosting (page 148).

Malted Espresso Cupcakes

Makes 12 cupcakes

I don't know if you've ever tried espresso and malt together, but they are an exceptional duo. So good, in fact, that a malted espresso cupcake was inevitable, and the critics are all abuzz about it.

Tip

You can find malted milk powder in most grocery stores, usually where the hot chocolate mix is found.

Variation

Stir $\frac{1}{2}$ cup (125 mL) coarsely chopped walnuts into the batter.

- **Preheat oven to 350°F (180°C)**
- **Muffin pan, lined with paper liners**

1$\frac{1}{2}$ cups	all-purpose flour	375 mL
1$\frac{1}{2}$ tsp	baking powder	7 mL
$\frac{1}{4}$ tsp	salt	1 mL
$\frac{1}{2}$ cup	malted milk powder (see Tip, left)	125 mL
$\frac{1}{4}$ cup	freshly brewed espresso or dark roast coffee	60 mL
1 cup	granulated sugar	250 mL
$\frac{1}{2}$ cup	unsalted butter, melted and cooled slightly	125 mL
2	eggs	2
	Frosting (see Frosting suggestions, below)	

1. In a small bowl, whisk together flour, baking powder and salt.

2. In a small bowl, whisk together malted milk powder and espresso until smooth.

3. In a large bowl, whisk together sugar, butter and eggs until smooth. Alternately whisk in flour mixture and espresso mixture, making three additions of flour mixture and two of espresso mixture, beating until smooth.

4. Scoop batter into prepared pan. Bake in preheated oven for 20 to 25 minutes or until golden brown and tops of cupcakes spring back when lightly touched. Let cool in pan on rack for 10 minutes. Remove from pan and let cool completely on rack. Top cooled cupcakes with frosting.

> **Frosting suggestions:** Malted Milk Espresso Icing (page 166) or Coffee Buttercream (page 155).

Cappuccino Cupcakes

Makes 12 cupcakes

I love the flavor of coffee and cinnamon in baked goods. And, as an added bonus, I can justify eating one of these delicious cupcakes for breakfast. That way, I feel like I'm having my morning cup of joe.

Tip

These cupcakes are delicious served warm with a scoop of Coffee Ice Cream (page 156) and a drizzle of Hot Fudge Sauce (page 163).

Variation

Omit the chocolate chips.

- **Preheat oven to 350°F (180°C)**
- **Muffin pan, lined with paper liners**

1 cup	all-purpose flour	250 mL
1 tbsp	finely ground coffee	15 mL
1 tsp	ground cinnamon	5 mL
½ tsp	baking powder	2 mL
¼ tsp	baking soda	1 mL
Pinch	salt	Pinch
1 tbsp	instant coffee granules	15 mL
1 tsp	warm water	5 mL
1 cup	granulated sugar	250 mL
¼ cup	canola oil	60 mL
1	egg	1
1 tsp	vanilla	5 mL
⅔ cup	sour cream	150 mL
½ cup	semisweet chocolate chips	125 mL
	Frosting (see Frosting suggestions, below)	

1. In a small bowl, whisk together flour, ground coffee, cinnamon, baking powder, baking soda and salt.

2. In another small bowl, whisk together instant coffee and warm water.

3. In a large bowl, whisk together sugar, oil and egg until smooth. Whisk in instant coffee mixture and vanilla. Alternately whisk in flour mixture and sour cream, making three additions of flour mixture and two of sour cream, beating until smooth. Mix in chocolate chips.

4. Scoop batter into prepared pan. Bake in preheated oven for 20 to 25 minutes or until tops of cupcakes spring back when lightly touched. Let cool in pan on rack for 10 minutes. Remove from pan and let cool completely on rack. Top cooled cupcakes with frosting.

> **Frosting suggestions:** Coffee Buttercream (page 155) or Chocolate Fudge Frosting (page 149).

Jay's Favorite Chocolate Cupcakes

I've been making these chocolate cupcakes for years, and they have never let me down. This recipe produces a lot of batter, which is an advantage when you're making cupcakes for a crowd.

Tip

The tops of these cupcakes sometimes cave in a little bit, but don't worry because the frosting covers it.

Variation

Omit the chocolate chips.

- Preheat oven to 350°F (180°C)
- 2 muffin pans, lined with paper liners

1½ cups	all-purpose flour	375 mL
¾ cup	unsweetened Dutch-process cocoa powder, sifted	175 mL
1 tsp	baking soda	5 mL
1 tsp	baking powder	5 mL
¼ tsp	salt	1 mL
1¾ cups	granulated sugar	425 mL
½ cup	canola oil	125 mL
2	eggs	2
1 tsp	vanilla	5 mL
1¼ cups	strong brewed coffee, at room temperature	300 mL
½ cup	semisweet chocolate chips	125 mL
	Frosting (see Frosting suggestions, below)	

1. In a small bowl, whisk together flour, cocoa powder, baking soda, baking powder and salt.

2. In a large bowl, whisk together sugar, oil and eggs until smooth. Whisk in vanilla. Alternately whisk in flour mixture and coffee, making three additions of flour mixture and two of coffee, beating until smooth. Stir in chocolate chips.

3. Scoop batter into prepared pans. Bake in preheated oven for 20 to 25 minutes or until tops of cupcakes spring back when lightly touched. Let cool in pans on rack for 10 minutes. Remove from pans and let cool completely on rack. Top cooled cupcakes with frosting.

> **Frosting suggestions:** Orange Cream Cheese Icing (page 168), Peanut Butter Frosting (page 169), Chocolate Fudge Frosting (page 149), or Coffee Ice Cream (page 156) and Hot Fudge Sauce (page 163).

Mocha Cupcakes

Here is yet another stimulating way to enjoy coffee combined with chocolate in one very delicious adult cupcake.

Tip

You can use instant espresso in place of the instant coffee granules.

Variation

Stir ½ cup (125 mL) semisweet chocolate chips into the batter.

- **Preheat oven to 350°F (180°C)**
- **Muffin pan, lined with paper liners**

¾ cup	all-purpose flour	175 mL
½ cup	unsweetened Dutch-process cocoa powder, sifted	125 mL
1 tbsp	finely ground coffee	15 mL
½ tsp	baking powder	2 mL
¼ tsp	baking soda	1 mL
Pinch	salt	Pinch
1 cup	granulated sugar	250 mL
⅓ cup	canola oil	75 mL
1	egg	1
⅓ cup	milk	75 mL
2 tbsp	instant coffee granules	30 mL
1 tsp	vanilla	5 mL
	Frosting (see Frosting suggestions, below)	

1. In a small bowl, whisk together flour, cocoa powder, ground coffee, baking powder, baking soda and salt.

2. In a large bowl, whisk together sugar, oil and egg until smooth. Add flour mixture, beating until combined.

3. In a bowl, whisk together milk, instant coffee and vanilla until coffee is dissolved. Add milk mixture to batter, beating until smooth.

4. Scoop batter into prepared pan. Bake in preheated oven for 20 to 25 minutes or until tops of cupcakes spring back when lightly touched. Let cool in pan on rack for 10 minutes. Remove from pan and let cool completely on rack. Top cooled cupcakes with frosting.

Frosting suggestions: Coffee Buttercream (page 155) or Chocolate Fudge Frosting (page 149).

Espresso Dark Brownie Cupcakes

This is an absolutely delicious, fudgy chocolate cupcake. It's a brownie and a cupcake all rolled up into one. When I need a chocolate fix, this cupcake fills the bill.

Tip

These cupcakes freeze well. Wrap them individually in plastic wrap and freeze them in resealable plastic freezer bags for up to 2 weeks.

Variation

Mix ⅓ to ½ cup (75 to 125 mL) chopped white chocolate into the batter.

- • **Preheat oven to 350°F (180°C)**
- • **2 muffin pans, lined with paper liners**

1 cup	unsalted butter, cut into pieces	250 mL
4 oz	unsweetened chocolate, chopped	125 g
1 cup	all-purpose flour	250 mL
¼ cup	unsweetened Dutch-process cocoa powder, sifted	60 mL
2 tbsp	finely ground espresso	30 mL
¼ tsp	salt	1 mL
1¾ cups	packed brown sugar	425 mL
½ cup	granulated sugar	125 mL
4	eggs	4
	Frosting (see Frosting suggestions, below)	

1. In a microwave-safe bowl, combine butter and chocolate. Microwave, uncovered, on High for 60 seconds, stirring every 30 seconds, or until butter is melted and chocolate is soft. Stir until smooth. Set aside and let cool slightly.

2. In a small bowl, whisk together flour, cocoa powder, espresso and salt.

3. In a large bowl, using an electric mixer, beat together brown and granulated sugars and reserved chocolate mixture until well combined. Add eggs, one at a time, beating well after each addition. Add flour mixture, mixing just until blended.

4. Scoop batter into prepared pans. Bake in preheated oven for 25 to 30 minutes or until a few moist crumbs cling to tester when inserted in center of cupcakes. Let cool in pans on rack for 10 minutes. Remove from pans and let cool completely on rack. Top cooled cupcakes with frosting.

> **Frosting suggestions:** Peanut Butter Frosting (page 169), Coffee Ice Cream (page 156) or Chocolate Fudge Frosting (page 149).

Earl Grey Cupcakes

Earl Grey tea adds a surprisingly delicious depth of flavor to these cupcakes.

Tip

These cupcakes are best served the day that they're made.

- **Preheat oven to 350°F (180°C)**
- **Muffin pan, lined with paper liners**

1½ cups	all-purpose flour	375 mL
¾ tsp	baking powder	3 mL
½ tsp	baking soda	2 mL
¼ tsp	salt	1 mL
2	Earl Grey tea bags or scant 1 tbsp (15 mL) loose tea	2
1¼ cups	granulated sugar	300 mL
6 tbsp	unsalted butter, at room temperature	90 mL
3	egg whites	3
1 tsp	grated orange zest	5 mL
¼ tsp	tangerine or orange oil or extract (see Tips, page 25)	1 mL
1 cup	buttermilk	250 mL
	Frosting (see Frosting suggestions, below)	

1. In a small bowl, whisk together flour, baking powder, baking soda and salt.

2. In a spice or coffee grinder, finely grind contents of tea bags. Add to flour mixture, mixing well.

3. In a large bowl, using an electric mixer, beat together sugar and butter until well combined. Add egg whites, one at a time, beating well after each addition. Add orange zest and tangerine oil, beating until smooth. Alternately beat in flour mixture and buttermilk, making three additions of flour mixture and two of buttermilk, beating until smooth.

4. Scoop batter into prepared pan. Bake in preheated oven for 20 to 25 minutes or until light golden and tops of cupcakes spring back when lightly touched. Let cool in pan on rack for 10 minutes. Remove from pan and let cool completely on rack. Top cooled cupcakes with frosting.

> **Frosting suggestions:** Orange Cream Cheese Icing (page 168) or Caramel Frosting (page 148).

Green Tea Cupcakes

Makes 12 cupcakes

What's the matcha with you? The green tea in this recipe makes a delicious and delicate batter. This is a perfect dessert to finish off an Asian meal or to serve as a playful Zen-style dessert. Use your imagination.

Tip

Look for matcha powder in Japanese markets or specialty tea shops.

Variation

Add ⅓ cup (75 mL) white chocolate chips to the batter.

- **Preheat oven to 350°F (180°C)**
- **Muffin pan, lined with paper liners**

1 cup	all-purpose flour	250 mL
1 tbsp	matcha green tea powder (see Tip, left)	15 mL
½ tsp	baking powder	2 mL
¼ tsp	baking soda	1 mL
Pinch	salt	Pinch
¾ cup	granulated sugar	175 mL
¼ cup	unsalted butter, at room temperature	60 mL
2	egg whites	2
⅔ cup	buttermilk	150 mL
	Easy Buttercream Frosting (see recipe, page 159)	

1. In a small bowl, whisk together flour, matcha powder, baking powder, baking soda and salt.

2. In a bowl, using an electric mixer, beat together sugar and butter until well combined. Add egg whites, one at a time, beating well after each addition. Alternately beat in flour mixture and buttermilk, making three additions of flour mixture and two of buttermilk, beating until smooth.

3. Scoop batter into prepared pan. Bake in preheated oven for 20 to 25 minutes or until tops of cupcakes spring back when lightly touched. Let cool in pan on rack for 10 minutes. Remove from pan and let cool completely on rack. Top cooled cupcakes with Easy Buttercream Frosting.

Kids' Corner

Candy Bar Cupcakes 76

Cookies and Cream Cupcakes 77

Ice Cream Cone Cupcakes 78

Confetti Cupcakes 79

Malted Milk Cupcakes 80

Coconut Cupcakes 82

Peppermint Candy Cupcakes 83

Toffee Cupcakes 84

White Cupcakes 85

Chocolate Mint Cupcakes 86

Pretty in Pink Cupcakes 87

Pink Lemonade Cupcakes 88

Candy Bar Cupcakes

My daughter, Sydney, LOVES these cupcakes. She said, "I love the way the chocolate melts in your mouth and I especially love to dig for the candy bar at the bottom of the cupcake. It's like finding hidden treasure."

Tip

Leftover Halloween candy bars are perfect for this recipe.

Variation

Substitute ½ cup (125 mL) whole candy-coated chocolate pieces, such as M&M's or Smarties, for the chopped candy bars.

- **Preheat oven to 350°F (180°C)**
- **Muffin pan, lined with paper liners**

1¼ cups	all-purpose flour	300 mL
½ cup	unsweetened Dutch-process cocoa powder, sifted	125 mL
¾ tsp	baking soda	3 mL
¼ tsp	salt	1 mL
1 cup	granulated sugar	250 mL
⅓ cup	canola oil	75 mL
1 tbsp	finely ground coffee	15 mL
1	egg	1
1 tsp	vanilla	5 mL
¾ cup	buttermilk	175 mL
2	large candy bars (such as Milky Way), cut into chunks (about 1 cup/250 mL)	2
	Frosting (see Frosting suggestions, below)	

1. In a small bowl, whisk together flour, cocoa powder, baking soda and salt.

2. In a large bowl, whisk together sugar, oil, coffee, egg and vanilla until smooth. Alternately whisk in flour mixture and buttermilk, making three additions of flour mixture and two of buttermilk, beating until smooth. Stir in chopped candy bars.

3. Scoop batter into prepared pan. Bake in preheated oven for 22 to 27 minutes or until tops of cupcakes spring back when lightly touched. Let cool in pan on rack for 10 minutes. Remove from pan and let cool completely on rack. Top cooled cupcakes with frosting.

> **Frosting suggestions:** Chocolate Fudge Frosting (page 149), Peanut Butter Frosting (page 169) or Caramel Frosting (page 148).

Cookies and Cream Cupcakes

Makes 12 cupcakes

You can find cookies and cream paired at ice cream parlors and in the freezers at local grocery and convenience stores alike. The combo also makes a dynamite cupcake with the delicious flavor of chocolaty cookies. I like to take it even further and top the cupcakes with Cookies and Cream Buttercream.

Variation

To make mini ice cream cakes, slice each cupcake in half horizontally. Spread 1 to 2 tbsp (15 to 30 mL) softened ice cream on each bottom half. Place cupcake top over ice cream and place on tray. Freeze cupcakes until almost frozen. Spread tops of cupcakes with frosting and return to freezer until solid and ready to serve.

- Preheat oven to 350°F (180°C)
- Muffin pan, lined with paper liners

1½ cups	all-purpose flour	375 mL
1½ tsp	baking powder	7 mL
¼ tsp	salt	1 mL
1 cup	granulated sugar	250 mL
½ cup	unsalted butter, melted and cooled slightly	125 mL
2	eggs	2
½ cup	milk	125 mL
10	chocolate sandwich cookies, smashed into small bits	10
	Frosting (see Frosting suggestions, below)	

1. In a small bowl, whisk together flour, baking powder and salt.

2. In a large bowl, whisk together sugar, butter and eggs until smooth. Alternately whisk in flour mixture and milk, making three additions of flour mixture and two of milk, beating until smooth. Add cookies, beating just until they're dispersed throughout batter. Do not overbeat.

3. Scoop batter into prepared pan. Bake in preheated oven for 20 to 25 minutes or until golden brown and tops of cupcakes spring back when lightly touched. Let cool in pan on rack for 10 minutes. Remove from pan and let cool completely on rack. Top cooled cupcakes with frosting.

> **Frosting suggestions:** Cookies and Cream Buttercream (page 157) or Chocolate Fudge Frosting (page 149).

Ice Cream Cone Cupcakes

Makes 12 cupcakes

Ice cream cones filled with cake and iced to look like real ice cream cones are a fun treat for kids and make a great alternative to ordinary birthday cake. They're a classic but still cool.

Tips

These cupcakes can be made up to 1 day ahead, but they taste best the day that they're made. Place unfrosted cupcakes in an airtight container and store at room temperature. Frost just before serving.

One package (18.25 oz/ 515 g) of cake mix will work in place of the cupcake batter. Prepare mix according to package directions, fill cones and bake as directed above.

- Preheat oven to 350°F (180°C)
- Muffin pan

1	recipe White Cupcake batter (see recipe, page 85)	1
12	flat-bottomed ice cream cones	12
	Frosting (see Frosting suggestions, below)	
	Sprinkles, candied cherries or other garnishes of choice	

1. Fill muffin pan with flat-bottomed ice cream cones. Fill each cone three-quarters full of cake batter. Bake in preheated oven for 25 to 30 minutes or until tops of cupcakes are golden brown and a tester inserted in center comes out clean.

2. Let cool completely in pan on rack. Top cooled cupcake cones with frosting. Sprinkle with garnishes.

> **Frosting suggestions:** Vanilla Cream Frosting (page 160), Peanut Butter Frosting (page 169) or Strawberry Cream Cheese Buttercream (page 172).

Confetti Cupcakes

I made up a batch of these cupcakes after wondering how the sprinkles would work in the batter instead of on top. They came out great, and all of the neighborhood children loved them, as well.

Tip

Look for colored ball-shaped sprinkles (sometimes called "hundreds and thousands") in the baking aisle of well-stocked grocery stores.

Variations

Substitute ½ tsp (2 mL) almond extract for the vanilla.

Top frosted cupcakes with more sprinkles for a colorful finish.

- **Preheat oven to 350°F (180°C)**
- **Muffin pan, lined with paper liners**

1 cup	all-purpose flour	250 mL
½ tsp	baking powder	2 mL
¼ tsp	baking soda	1 mL
Pinch	salt	Pinch
¾ cup	granulated sugar	175 mL
¼ cup	unsalted butter, at room temperature	60 mL
2	egg whites	2
1 tsp	vanilla	5 mL
⅔ cup	buttermilk	150 mL
2 tbsp	nonpareils or colored sprinkles (see Tip, left)	30 mL
	Frosting (see Frosting suggestions, below)	

1. In a small bowl, whisk together flour, baking powder, baking soda and salt.

2. In a bowl, using an electric mixer, beat together sugar and butter until well combined. Add egg whites, one at a time, beating well after each addition. Beat in vanilla. Alternately beat in flour mixture and buttermilk, making three additions of flour mixture and two of buttermilk, beating until smooth. Mix in nonpareils.

3. Scoop batter into prepared pan. Bake in preheated oven for 20 to 25 minutes or until tops of cupcakes spring back when lightly touched. Let cool in pan on rack for 10 minutes. Remove from pan and let cool completely on rack. Top cooled cupcakes with frosting.

> **Frosting suggestions:** Easy Buttercream Frosting (page 159) or Vanilla Cream Frosting (page 160).

Malted Milk Cupcakes

This is one of my children's favorites for obvious reasons. They love to bring them in their school lunches to share with their friends. Once word of these cupcakes spread around school, my kids were asking for them daily.

Tips

You can find malted milk powder in most grocery stores, usually where the hot chocolate mix is found.

If it's too difficult to cut the malted milk balls in half with a knife, you can place them in a resealable bag and break them with a mallet.

- Preheat oven to 350°F (180°C)
- Muffin pan, lined with paper liners

1½ cups	all-purpose flour	375 mL
1½ tsp	baking powder	7 mL
¼ tsp	salt	1 mL
1 cup	granulated sugar	250 mL
½ cup	unsalted butter, melted and cooled slightly	125 mL
2	eggs	2
⅓ cup	milk	75 mL
2 tbsp	malted milk powder (see Tips, left)	30 mL
1 cup	chocolate-covered malted milk balls, halved (see Tips, left)	250 mL
	Frosting (see Frosting suggestions, right)	

1. In a small bowl, whisk together flour, baking powder and salt.

2. In a large bowl, whisk together sugar, butter and eggs until smooth. In another bowl, whisk together milk and malted milk powder.

3. Alternately whisk flour mixture and milk mixture into butter mixture, making three additions of flour mixture and two of milk mixture, beating until smooth. Stir in malted milk balls.

4. Scoop batter into prepared pan. Bake in preheated oven for 20 to 25 minutes or until golden brown and tops of cupcakes spring back when lightly touched. Let cool in pan on rack for 10 minutes. Remove from pan and let cool completely on rack. Top cooled cupcakes with frosting.

> **Frosting suggestions:** Chocolate Fudge Frosting (page 149) or Malted Milk Espresso Icing (page 166).

Coconut Cupcakes

This cupcake is light, bright, airy and white, with a hint of coconut for a tongue-titillating taste of the tropics.

Tip

These cupcakes are best served the day that they're made.

Variation

Add ½ cup (125 mL) semisweet chocolate chips to the batter.

- **Preheat oven to 350°F (180°C)**
- **Muffin pan, lined with paper liners**

1½ cups	all-purpose flour	375 mL
½ cup	sweetened flaked coconut, toasted and cooled (see Tips, page 108)	125 mL
¾ tsp	baking powder	3 mL
½ tsp	baking soda	2 mL
¼ tsp	salt	1 mL
1¼ cups	granulated sugar	300 mL
6 tbsp	unsalted butter, at room temperature	90 mL
3	egg whites	3
1 cup	buttermilk	250 mL
	Frosting (see Frosting suggestions, below)	

1. In a small bowl, whisk together flour, coconut, baking powder, baking soda and salt.

2. In a bowl, using an electric mixer, beat together sugar and butter until well combined. Add egg whites, one at a time, beating well after each addition. Alternately beat in flour mixture and buttermilk, making three additions of flour mixture and two of buttermilk, beating just until smooth.

3. Scoop batter into prepared pan. Bake in preheated oven for 20 to 25 minutes or until tops of cupcakes spring back when lightly touched. Let cool in pan on rack for 10 minutes. Remove from pan and let cool completely on rack. Top cooled cupcakes with frosting.

> **Frosting suggestions:** Chocolate Fudge Frosting (page 149), Cream Cheese Icing (page 158) or Rum Buttercream (page 171).

Peppermint Candy Cupcakes

Makes 12 cupcakes

My husband, Jay (you can't take the kid out of him!), loves these cupcakes. Crushed candy canes stirred into the batter melt while baking, then crystallize slightly as they cool. If you like peppermint candies, you'll love these cupcakes.

Tip

If you can't find candy canes, substitute hard peppermint candies (crush up enough so that you have ⅓ cup/75 mL).

Variation

Add ½ cup (125 mL) coarsely chopped bittersweet or white chocolate to the batter.

- **Preheat oven to 350°F (180°C)**
- **Muffin pan, lined with paper liners**

1 cup	all-purpose flour	250 mL
½ tsp	baking powder	2 mL
¼ tsp	baking soda	1 mL
Pinch	salt	Pinch
⅓ cup	finely chopped candy canes (about 4 medium)	75 mL
¾ cup	granulated sugar	175 mL
⅓ cup	unsalted butter, at room temperature	75 mL
2	egg whites	2
½ cup	buttermilk	125 mL
	Frosting (see Frosting suggestions, below)	

1. In a bowl, whisk together flour, baking powder, baking soda and salt. Stir in chopped candy canes.

2. In a bowl, using an electric mixer, beat together sugar and butter until well combined. Add egg whites, one at a time, beating well after each addition. Alternately beat in flour mixture and buttermilk, making three additions of flour mixture and two of buttermilk, beating until smooth.

3. Scoop batter into prepared pan. Bake in preheated oven for 20 to 25 minutes or until tops of cupcakes spring back when lightly touched. Let cool in pan on rack for 10 minutes. Remove from pan and let cool completely on rack. Top cooled cupcakes with frosting.

> **Frosting suggestions:** Chocolate Fudge Frosting (page 149) or Easy Buttercream Frosting (page 159).

Toffee Cupcakes

Makes 12 cupcakes

My daughter, Sydney, thinks that life can't get much better than toffee. So I created this cupcake for her, folding chopped toffee bits into the cupcake batter. The toffee bits partially melt, permeating the cupcake with their buttery flavor. She's been known to do dishes for this cupcake.

Tip

You can find toffee bits in bags in most well-stocked grocery stores.

Variation

Add crushed chocolate-covered toffee bars to the batter instead of the toffee bits or 1/3 cup (75 mL) semisweet chocolate chips along with the toffee bits.

- **Preheat oven to 350°F (180°C)**
- **Muffin pan, lined with paper liners**

1 cup	all-purpose flour	250 mL
1/2 tsp	baking powder	2 mL
1/4 tsp	baking soda	1 mL
Pinch	salt	Pinch
3/4 cup	packed brown sugar	175 mL
1/4 cup	unsalted butter, at room temperature	60 mL
2	egg whites	2
2/3 cup	buttermilk	150 mL
2/3 cup	toffee bits (see Tip, left)	150 mL
	Frosting (see Frosting suggestions, below)	

1. In a small bowl, whisk together flour, baking powder, baking soda and salt.

2. In a bowl, using an electric mixer, beat together brown sugar and butter until well combined. Add egg whites, one at a time, beating well after each addition. Alternately beat in flour mixture and buttermilk, making three additions of flour mixture and two of buttermilk, beating until smooth. Add toffee bits, beating until smooth.

3. Scoop batter into prepared pan. Bake in preheated oven for 20 to 25 minutes or until tops of cupcakes spring back when lightly touched. Let cool in pan on rack for 10 minutes. Remove from pan and let cool completely on rack. Top cooled cupcakes with frosting.

> **Frosting suggestions:** Caramel Frosting (page 148), Easy Buttercream Frosting (page 159) or Chocolate Fudge Frosting (page 149).

White Cupcakes

From time to time, you will find yourself in need of a great basic vanilla cupcake recipe. Look no further: this recipe is everything a white cupcake should be. It's perfect for everything from children's birthday parties to weddings.

Tip

These cupcakes are best frosted and served the day that they're made.

Variation

Substitute vanilla for the almond extract.

- **Preheat oven to 350°F (180°C)**
- **Muffin pan, lined with paper liners**

1 cup	all-purpose flour	250 mL
½ tsp	baking powder	2 mL
¼ tsp	baking soda	1 mL
Pinch	salt	Pinch
¾ cup	granulated sugar	175 mL
¼ cup	unsalted butter, at room temperature	60 mL
2	egg whites	2
1 tsp	almond extract	5 mL
⅔ cup	buttermilk	150 mL
	Frosting (see Frosting suggestions, below)	

1. In a small bowl, whisk together flour, baking powder, baking soda and salt.

2. In a bowl, using an electric mixer, beat together sugar and butter until well combined. Add egg whites, one at a time, beating well after each addition. Mix in almond extract. Alternately beat in flour mixture and buttermilk, making three additions of flour mixture and two of buttermilk, beating until smooth.

3. Scoop batter into prepared pan. Bake in preheated oven for 20 to 25 minutes or until tops of cupcakes spring back when lightly touched. Let cool in pan on rack for 10 minutes. Remove from pan and let cool completely on rack. Top cooled cupcakes with frosting.

> **Frosting suggestions:** Chocolate Glaze (page 150), Chocolate Fudge Frosting (page 149), Cookies and Cream Buttercream (page 157) or Strawberry Cream Cheese Buttercream (page 172).

Chocolate Mint Cupcakes

Let me just say that these little cakes are fudgy and delicious! My son, Noah, tells me that the flavor reminds him of his favorite mint chocolate chip ice cream. If these cupcakes cave in somewhat on top as they cool, the frosting will hide it.

Tip

These cupcakes are best frosted and served the day that they're made.

Variation

Substitute chocolate mint chips or a chopped chocolate mint candy bar for the semisweet chocolate chips.

- **Preheat oven to 350°F (180°C)**
- **Muffin pan, lined with paper liners**

¾ cup	all-purpose flour	175 mL
⅓ cup	unsweetened Dutch-process cocoa powder, sifted	75 mL
½ tsp	baking soda	2 mL
½ tsp	baking powder	2 mL
Pinch	salt	Pinch
¾ cup	granulated sugar	175 mL
⅓ cup	canola oil	75 mL
1	egg	1
¼ tsp	peppermint extract	1 mL
½ cup	milk	125 mL
½ cup	semisweet chocolate chips	125 mL
	Frosting (see Frosting suggestions, below)	

1. In a small bowl, whisk together flour, cocoa powder, baking soda, baking powder and salt.

2. In a large bowl, whisk together sugar, oil and egg until smooth. Add peppermint extract, mixing well. Alternately whisk in flour mixture and milk, making three additions of flour mixture and two of milk, beating until smooth. Stir in chocolate chips.

3. Scoop batter into prepared pan. Bake in preheated oven for 20 to 25 minutes or until tops of cupcakes spring back when lightly touched. Let cool in pan on rack for 10 minutes. Remove from pan and let cool completely on rack. Top cooled cupcakes with frosting.

> **Frosting suggestions:** Chocolate Fudge Frosting (page 149); Chocolate Glaze (page 150); or Easy Buttercream Frosting (page 159, see Variation with peppermint extract).

Pretty in Pink Cupcakes

Makes 12 cupcakes

Puréed fresh strawberries give these cupcakes a pretty pink color. Little girls go especially crazy for these pink treats.

Tip

You can add a drop of red or pink food coloring to the batter along with the strawberries for a slightly brighter shade of pink.

- **Preheat oven to 350°F (180°C)**
- **Muffin pan, lined with paper liners**

1 cup	all-purpose flour	250 mL
½ tsp	baking powder	2 mL
¼ tsp	baking soda	1 mL
Pinch	salt	Pinch
¾ cup	granulated sugar	175 mL
¼ cup	unsalted butter, at room temperature	60 mL
2	egg whites	2
⅓ cup	puréed fresh strawberries (about 4 large)	75 mL
⅔ cup	buttermilk	150 mL
	Frosting (see Frosting suggestions, below)	

1. In a small bowl, whisk together flour, baking powder, baking soda and salt.

2. In a bowl, using an electric mixer, beat together sugar and butter until well combined. Add egg whites, one at a time, beating well after each addition. Add puréed strawberries, mixing well. Alternately beat in flour mixture and buttermilk, making three additions of flour mixture and two of buttermilk, beating just until smooth.

3. Scoop batter into prepared pan. Bake in preheated oven for 20 to 25 minutes or until tops of cupcakes spring back when lightly touched. Let cool in pan on rack for 10 minutes. Remove from pan and let cool completely on rack. Top cooled cupcakes with frosting.

> **Frosting suggestions:** Easy Buttercream Frosting (page 159) or Strawberry Cream Cheese Buttercream (page 172).

Pink Lemonade Cupcakes

Makes 10 cupcakes

I was trying to imagine a great kid-friendly cupcake when my mother suggested pink lemonade. Brilliant! I immediately started picturing summertime lemonade stands, but instead of glasses of lemonade, there were trays of perfect pink-colored cupcakes with a delectable lemon tang. Anyone up for a lemonade cupcake stand?

Tip

If you can't find frozen pink lemonade concentrate, substitute regular lemonade concentrate and add an extra drop or two of red food coloring to the batter for the pink color.

- **Preheat oven to 350°F (180°C)**
- **Muffin pan, lined with paper liners**

1 cup	all-purpose flour	250 mL
½ tsp	baking powder	2 mL
¼ tsp	baking soda	1 mL
Pinch	salt	Pinch
½ cup	granulated sugar	125 mL
¼ cup	canola oil	60 mL
2	egg whites	2
⅓ cup	thawed frozen pink lemonade concentrate	75 mL
¼ cup	buttermilk	60 mL
2 to 3	drops red food coloring	2 to 3
	Frosting (see Frosting suggestions, below)	

1. In a small bowl, combine flour, baking powder, baking soda and salt.

2. In a large bowl, whisk together sugar, oil, egg whites and lemonade concentrate. Alternately whisk in flour mixture and buttermilk, making three additions of flour mixture and two of buttermilk, beating just until smooth. Add just enough food coloring to turn the batter a light shade of pink.

3. Scoop batter into prepared pan. Bake in preheated oven for 20 to 25 minutes or until tops of cupcakes spring back when lightly touched. Let cool in pan on rack for 10 minutes. Remove from pan and let cool completely on rack. Top cooled cupcakes with frosting.

> **Frosting Suggestions:** Easy Buttercream Frosting (page 159) with a drop of red food coloring added to make it pink, if desired; Cream Cheese Icing (page 158); or Vegan Lemon Glaze (page 181).

Spice It Up

Anise Cupcakes 90

Banana Nutmeg Cupcakes 91

Cardamom Plum Cupcakes 92

Carrot Cupcakes 93

Chocolate Chile Cupcakes 94

French Toast Cupcakes 95

Ginger Cupcakes 96

Maple Raisin Cupcakes 97

Pumpkin Cupcakes 98

Spice Cupcakes 99

Zucchini Chocolate Spice Cupcakes 100

Spiced Peach Cupcakes 101

Applesauce Cupcakes 102

Chai Cupcakes 104

Anise Cupcakes

Years ago a fellow foodie, Arlene Gould, told me that when she made anise cookies, she would add the contents of a licorice tea bag to the batter. Well, when my husband, Jay, suggested that I make a licorice cupcake, I knew exactly where to begin. These are really delicious, with a subtle anise flavor.

Variation

Sprinkle tops of frosted cupcakes with sliced almonds.

- **Preheat oven to 350°F (180°C)**
- **Muffin pan, lined with paper liners**

1½ cups	all-purpose flour	375 mL
1½ tsp	baking powder	7 mL
¼ tsp	salt	1 mL
2	licorice tea bags or scant 1 tbsp (15 mL) loose tea	2
1 cup	granulated sugar	250 mL
½ cup	unsalted butter, melted and cooled slightly	125 mL
2	eggs	2
1 tsp	anise extract	5 mL
½ cup	milk	125 mL
	Frosting (see Frosting suggestions, below)	

1. In a small bowl, whisk together flour, baking powder and salt.

2. In a spice or coffee grinder, finely grind contents of tea bags. Stir into flour mixture.

3. In a large bowl, whisk together sugar, butter, eggs and anise extract until smooth. Alternately whisk in flour mixture and milk, making three additions of flour mixture and two of milk, beating until smooth.

4. Scoop batter into prepared pan. Bake in preheated oven for 22 to 27 minutes or until golden brown and tops of cupcakes spring back when lightly touched. Let cool in pan on rack for 10 minutes. Remove from pan and let cool completely on rack. Top cooled cupcakes with frosting.

> **Frosting suggestions:** Easy Buttercream Frosting (page 159) or Cream Cheese Icing (page 158).

Banana Nutmeg Cupcakes

Whisk together bananas and nutmeg and the sum is tastier than the parts. I love this flavor duo together for the simple reason that it's totally delicious.

Variation

Add ½ cup (125 mL) chopped milk chocolate to the batter.

- **Preheat oven to 350°F (180°C)**
- **Muffin pan, lined with paper liners**

1½ cups	all-purpose flour	375 mL
1½ tsp	baking powder	7 mL
½ tsp	ground nutmeg	2 mL
¼ tsp	salt	1 mL
1 cup	granulated sugar	250 mL
½ cup	unsalted butter, melted and cooled slightly	125 mL
2	eggs	2
½ cup	milk	125 mL
2	bananas, sliced	2
	Granulated sugar	
	Frosting (see Frosting suggestions, below), optional	

1. In a small bowl, whisk together flour, baking powder, nutmeg and salt.

2. In a large bowl, whisk together sugar, butter and eggs until smooth. Alternately whisk in flour mixture and milk, making three additions of flour mixture and two of milk, beating until smooth.

3. Scoop batter into prepared pan. Top each cupcake with three overlapping slices of banana. Sprinkle a pinch of sugar over top of each cupcake.

4. Bake in preheated oven for 22 to 27 minutes or until golden brown and a tester inserted in the center of cupcake comes out clean. Let cool in pan on rack for 10 minutes. Remove from pan and let cool completely on rack. Top cooled cupcakes with frosting, if using.

> **Frosting suggestions:** Cream Cheese Icing (page 158), Chocolate Fudge Frosting (page 149) or Easy Buttercream Frosting (page 159).

Cardamom Plum Cupcakes

This cupcake is delicious, with the light peppery taste of cardamom balanced by the sweet-tart taste of roasted plums. My mom brought over a bag of just-picked juicy ripe plums from her tree. Naturally, I was very excited to put them to good cupcake use.

Tip

Don't substitute dried plums (prunes) for the fresh — they won't give the same result.

Variation

Substitute ground allspice for the cardamom.

- **Preheat oven to 350°F (180°C)**
- **Muffin pan, lined with paper liners**

1½ cups	all-purpose flour	375 mL
1½ tsp	baking powder	7 mL
¾ tsp	ground cardamom	3 mL
¼ tsp	salt	1 mL
1 cup	granulated sugar	250 mL
½ cup	unsalted butter, melted and cooled slightly	125 mL
2	eggs	2
⅓ cup	milk	75 mL
3	red plums, pitted and thinly sliced	3
	Frosting (see Frosting suggestions, below), optional	

1. In a small bowl, whisk together flour, baking powder, cardamom and salt.

2. In a large bowl, whisk together sugar, butter and eggs until smooth. Alternately whisk in flour mixture and milk, making three additions of flour mixture and two of milk, beating until smooth.

3. Scoop batter into prepared pan. Arrange two or three slices of plum on top of each cupcake.

4. Bake in preheated oven for 22 to 27 minutes or until a tester inserted in center of cupcake comes out clean. Let cool in pan on rack for 10 minutes. Remove from pan and let cool completely on rack. Top cooled cupcakes with frosting, if using.

> **Frosting suggestions:** Easy Buttercream Frosting (page 159) or Honey Cream Cheese Frosting (page 162).

Carrot Cupcakes

This recipe has all the wonderful attributes of a large cake packed into a pint-size treat.

Tip
These cupcakes freeze well. Wrap them individually in plastic wrap and freeze in an airtight container for up to 2 weeks.

Variation
Substitute ½ cup (125 mL) raisins for the coconut.

- Preheat oven to 350°F (180°C)
- Muffin pan, lined with paper liners

1 cup	all-purpose flour	250 mL
1 tsp	baking soda	5 mL
1 tsp	ground cinnamon	5 mL
Pinch	salt	Pinch
1 cup	granulated sugar	250 mL
½ cup	canola oil	125 mL
2	eggs	2
1	can (8 oz/227 mL) crushed pineapple in juice, drained well	1
1 cup	packed grated carrots	250 mL
½ cup	loosely packed sweetened flaked coconut	125 mL
	Frosting (see Frosting suggestions, below)	

1. In a small bowl, whisk together flour, baking soda, cinnamon and salt.

2. In a large bowl, whisk together sugar, oil and eggs until smooth. Add pineapple, carrots and coconut, beating until mixed. Add flour mixture, beating just until blended.

3. Scoop batter into prepared pans. Bake in preheated oven for 22 minutes or until golden brown and tops of cupcakes spring back when lightly touched. Let cool in pan on rack for 10 minutes. Remove from pan and let cool completely on rack. Top cooled cupcakes with frosting.

> **Frosting suggestions:** Cream Cheese Icing (page 158), Ginger Cream Cheese Icing (page 161) or Caramel Frosting (page 148).

Chocolate Chile Cupcakes

I'm sure you're wondering how chocolate and chile go together, but let me assure you that it is a match made in heaven. You don't taste the chile; you feel only a slight amount of heat from it. So what you wind up with is a deep chocolate flavor with a little kick and a slight jump in your heart rate.

Tip

These are best served the day that they're made.

Variation

Substitute white chocolate chips for the semisweet chocolate chips.

- **Preheat oven to 350°F (180°C)**
- **Muffin pan, lined with paper liners**

1¼ cups	all-purpose flour	300 mL
½ cup	unsweetened Dutch-process cocoa powder, sifted	125 mL
1 tbsp	ancho chile powder or 1 tsp (5 mL) chipotle chile powder	15 mL
2 tsp	finely ground coffee	10 mL
¾ tsp	baking soda	3 mL
¼ tsp	salt	1 mL
1 cup	granulated sugar	250 mL
⅓ cup	canola oil	75 mL
1	egg	1
1 tsp	vanilla	5 mL
¾ cup	buttermilk	175 mL
1 tbsp	instant coffee granules	15 mL
½ cup	semisweet chocolate chips	125 mL
	Frosting (see Frosting suggestions, below)	

1. In a small bowl, whisk together flour, cocoa powder, chile powder, ground coffee, baking soda and salt.

2. In a large bowl, whisk together sugar, oil, egg and vanilla until smooth. In a separate bowl, stir together buttermilk and instant coffee.

3. Alternately whisk flour mixture and buttermilk mixture into oil mixture, making three additions of flour mixture and two of buttermilk mixture, beating until smooth. Mix in chocolate chips.

4. Scoop batter into prepared pan. Bake for 22 to 27 minutes or until tops of cupcakes spring back when lightly touched. Let cool in pan on rack for 10 minutes. Remove from pan and let cool completely on rack. Top cooled cupcakes with frosting.

> **Frosting suggestions:** Chocolate Fudge Frosting (page 149) or Chocolate Glaze (page 150).

French Toast Cupcakes

I love French toast and thought that it would be fun to combine the flavors of cinnamon and maple in a cupcake. It's delicious topped with Cream Cheese Icing.

Tip

Make and frost these cupcakes the same day that you plan on serving them.

Variation

Omit the frosting and sprinkle the tops of the unbaked cupcakes with ground cinnamon or cinnamon sugar.

- **Preheat oven to 350°F (180°C)**
- **Muffin pan, lined with paper liners**

1½ cups	all-purpose flour	375 mL
1½ tsp	baking powder	7 mL
½ tsp	ground cinnamon	2 mL
¼ tsp	salt	1 mL
1 cup	granulated sugar	250 mL
½ cup	unsalted butter, melted and cooled slightly	125 mL
2	eggs	2
1 tsp	maple extract	5 mL
½ cup	milk	125 mL
	Frosting (see Frosting suggestions, below)	

1. In a small bowl, whisk together flour, baking powder, cinnamon and salt.

2. In a large bowl, whisk together sugar, butter and eggs until smooth. Whisk in maple extract. Alternately whisk in flour mixture and milk, making three additions of flour mixture and two of milk, beating until smooth.

3. Scoop batter into prepared pan. Bake in preheated oven for 20 to 25 minutes or until golden brown and tops of cupcakes spring back when lightly touched. Let cool in pan on rack for 10 minutes. Remove from pan and let cool completely on rack. Top cooled cupcakes with frosting.

> **Frosting suggestions:** Cream Cheese Icing (page 158) or Maple Buttercream (page 167).

Ginger Cupcakes

Makes 12 cupcakes

My mom absolutely flipped for this cupcake, which is full of the sweet and spicy flavor of ginger. For die-hard ginger fans, you can top these very gingery cupcakes with Ginger Cream Cheese Icing.

Tip

The easiest ways to chop the candied ginger is either with a sharp chef's knife or in a food processor.

Variation

Add ½ cup (125 mL) raisins to the batter.

- **Preheat oven to 350°F (180°C)**
- **Muffin pan, lined with paper liners**

1½ cups	all-purpose flour	375 mL
1 tbsp	ground ginger	15 mL
1 tsp	baking powder	5 mL
¼ tsp	salt	1 mL
¾ cup	finely chopped candied ginger (see Tip, left)	175 mL
1¼ cups	granulated sugar	300 mL
½ cup	unsalted butter, at room temperature	125 mL
3	eggs	3
¾ cup	milk	175 mL
	Frosting (see Frosting suggestions, below)	

1. In a small bowl, whisk together flour, ginger, baking powder and salt. Stir in candied ginger.

2. In a large bowl, using an electric mixer, beat together sugar and butter until well combined. Add eggs, one at a time, beating well after each addition. Alternately beat in flour mixture and milk, making three additions of flour mixture and two of milk, beating until smooth.

3. Scoop batter into prepared pan. Bake in preheated oven for 23 to 28 minutes or until golden brown and tops of cupcakes spring back when lightly touched. Let cool in pan on rack for 10 minutes. Remove from pan and let cool completely on rack. Top cooled cupcakes with frosting.

> **Frosting suggestions:** Caramel Frosting (page 148), Ginger Cream Cheese Icing (page 161) or Cream Cheese Icing (page 158).

Maple Raisin Cupcakes

Psst! Calling all recipe procrastinators. The food processor makes this cupcake batter quicker than a cake mix, and the cupcakes come out delicious and full flavored as quick as you can say "Pulse." Just do it!

Tip

If you don't have a food processor, you can beat the batter together with a hand or stand mixer following the method for Ginger Cupcakes (page 96).

Variation

Omit the raisins.

- **Preheat oven to 350°F (180°C)**
- **Muffin pan, lined with paper liners**

1 cup	cake flour, sifted	250 mL
1 tsp	baking powder	5 mL
Pinch	salt	Pinch
¾ cup	granulated sugar	175 mL
½ cup	unsalted butter, at room temperature	125 mL
2	eggs	2
1½ tsp	maple extract	7 mL
¼ cup	milk	60 mL
½ cup	raisins	125 mL
	Maple Buttercream (see recipe, page 167)	

1. In a food processor fitted with a metal blade, pulse flour, baking powder and salt until mixed.

2. Add sugar and butter, pulsing several times until incorporated. Add eggs and maple extract, pulsing until smooth. Add milk and pulse until combined. Remove metal blade and stir in raisins.

3. Scoop batter into prepared pan. Bake in preheated oven for 20 to 25 minutes or until golden brown and tops of cupcakes spring back when lightly touched. Let cool in pan on rack for 10 minutes. Remove from pan and let cool completely on rack. Top cooled cupcakes with Maple Buttercream.

Pumpkin Cupcakes

I am a pumpkin nut, putting it in everything from pancakes to cookies to cakes to ice cream. So, naturally, I have created a delicious pumpkin cupcake, which is awesome any time of the year. Try it topped with Rum Buttercream or Caramel Frosting.

Tip

I like to stock up on canned pumpkin during the fall, when it's easy to find in the grocery stores. Some markets only stock it in the winter months.

Variation

Add ½ cup (125 mL) raisins to the batter.

- **Preheat oven to 350°F (180°C)**
- **Muffin pan, lined with paper liners**

1½ cups	all-purpose flour	375 mL
1 tsp	ground cinnamon	5 mL
¾ tsp	baking powder	3 mL
¾ tsp	baking soda	3 mL
½ tsp	ground allspice	2 mL
½ tsp	ground nutmeg	2 mL
¼ tsp	salt	1 mL
1½ cups	granulated sugar	375 mL
½ cup	canola oil	125 mL
2	eggs	2
1 cup	canned pumpkin purée (not pumpkin pie filling)	250 mL
2 tbsp	cream sherry	30 mL
	Frosting (see Frosting suggestions, below)	

1. In a small bowl, whisk together flour, cinnamon, baking powder, baking soda, allspice, nutmeg and salt.

2. In a large bowl, whisk together sugar, oil and eggs until smooth. Add pumpkin and sherry, beating well. Add flour mixture, beating until smooth.

3. Scoop batter into prepared pan. Bake in preheated oven for 22 to 27 minutes or until tops of cupcakes spring back when lightly touched. Let cool in pan on rack for 10 minutes. Remove from pan and let cool completely on rack. Top cooled cupcakes with frosting.

> **Frosting suggestions:** Maple Buttercream (page 167), Rum Buttercream (page 171), Cream Cheese Icing (page 158) or Caramel Frosting (page 148).

Spice Cupcakes

Makes 12 cupcakes

This cupcake is a favorite of my family that I love to make in the fall. Something about the fall weather screams "spice cake" to me. The spices make you feel like you're biting into something earthy, organic and satisfying.

Variation

Add ⅓ cup (75 mL) semisweet chocolate chips to the batter.

- **Preheat oven to 350°F (180°C)**
- **Muffin pan, lined with paper liners**

1 cup	all-purpose flour	250 mL
½ tsp	baking powder	2 mL
½ tsp	ground allspice	2 mL
½ tsp	ground cinnamon	2 mL
¼ tsp	baking soda	1 mL
¼ tsp	ground nutmeg	1 mL
¼ tsp	salt	1 mL
½ cup	raisins	125 mL
¾ cup	granulated sugar	175 mL
¼ cup	unsalted butter, at room temperature	60 mL
2 tbsp	fancy molasses	30 mL
1	egg	1
⅔ cup	buttermilk	150 mL
	Frosting (see Frosting suggestions, below)	

1. In a small bowl, whisk together flour, baking powder, allspice, cinnamon, baking soda, nutmeg and salt. Stir in raisins.

2. In a bowl, using an electric mixer, beat together sugar and butter until well combined. Add molasses and egg, beating well. Alternately beat in flour mixture and buttermilk, making three additions of flour mixture and two of buttermilk, beating until smooth.

3. Scoop batter into prepared pan. Bake in preheated oven for 20 to 25 minutes or until tops of cupcakes spring back when lightly touched. Let cool in pan on rack for 10 minutes. Remove from pan and let cool completely on rack. Top cooled cupcakes with frosting.

> **Frosting suggestions:** Ginger Cream Cheese Icing (page 161), Cream Cheese Icing (page 158) or Maple Buttercream (page 167).

Zucchini Chocolate Spice Cupcakes

Chocolate zucchini cake was one of the biggest sellers when my husband, Jay, and I had our bakery. So it was impossible to not include a version of that cake in this book. I hope that you enjoy it as much as we do.

Tip

Don't use overly ripe zucchini for this recipe, because they tend to get soft and will add too much moisture to the cupcakes.

Variation

Omit the chocolate chips.

- • **Preheat oven to 350°F (180°C)**
- • **Muffin pan, lined with paper liners**

1 cup	all-purpose flour	250 mL
¼ cup	unsweetened Dutch-process cocoa powder, sifted	60 mL
½ tsp	baking soda	2 mL
½ tsp	baking powder	2 mL
½ tsp	ground cinnamon	2 mL
¼ tsp	ground nutmeg	1 mL
¼ tsp	ground allspice	1 mL
Pinch	salt	Pinch
1 cup	granulated sugar	250 mL
½ cup	canola oil	125 mL
2	eggs	2
½ tsp	vanilla	2 mL
1½ cups	lightly packed shredded zucchini (about 2 small zucchini)	375 mL
½ cup	semisweet chocolate chips	125 mL
	Frosting (see Frosting suggestions, below)	

1. In a small bowl, whisk together flour, cocoa powder, baking soda, baking powder, cinnamon, nutmeg, allspice and salt.

2. In a large bowl, whisk together sugar, oil and eggs until smooth. Beat in vanilla. Add flour mixture, beating until smooth. Mix in zucchini and chocolate chips.

3. Scoop batter into prepared pan. Bake in preheated oven for 25 to 30 minutes or until tops of cupcakes spring back when lightly touched. Let cool in pan on rack for 10 minutes. Remove from pan and let cool completely on rack. Top cooled cupcakes with frosting.

> **Frosting suggestions:** Chocolate Glaze (page 150), Chocolate Fudge Frosting (page 149) or Cream Cheese Icing (page 158).

Spiced Peach Cupcakes

I love to go to the farmer's market at the beginning of summer and smell all of the wonderfully fragrant fruit. But I go really crazy for the sweet, juicy June peaches. So I decided to take those sweet, fragrant flavors of summer and put them into a cupcake.

Tip

I like to keep canned peaches on hand during the winter, for when the mood strikes me to bake up a batch of these cupcakes.

Variation

Serve these cupcakes with a scoop of Vanilla Ice Cream (page 173).

- **Preheat oven to 350°F (180°C)**
- **Muffin pan, lined with paper liners**

1½ cups	all-purpose flour	375 mL
1½ tsp	baking powder	7 mL
½ tsp	ground cinnamon	2 mL
½ tsp	ground allspice	2 mL
¼ tsp	salt	1 mL
1 cup	granulated sugar	250 mL
½ cup	unsalted butter, melted and cooled slightly	125 mL
2	eggs	2
⅓ cup	milk	75 mL
¾ cup	sliced peeled pitted peaches (if canned, drain well)	175 mL
	Frosting (see Frosting suggestions, below)	

1. In a small bowl, whisk together flour, baking powder, cinnamon, allspice and salt.

2. In a large bowl, whisk together sugar, butter and eggs until smooth. Alternately whisk in flour mixture and milk, making three additions of flour mixture and two of milk, beating until smooth. Stir in peaches.

3. Scoop batter into prepared pan. Bake in preheated oven for 22 to 27 minutes or until golden brown and tops of cupcakes spring back when lightly touched. Let cool in pan on rack for 10 minutes. Remove from pan and let cool completely on rack. Top cooled cupcakes with frosting.

> **Frosting suggestions:** Caramel Frosting (page 148), Honey Cream Cheese Frosting (page 162) or Easy Buttercream Frosting (page 159).

Applesauce Cupcakes

Applesauce rules! I love it
so much that this cupcake
was a given. When you're in
the mood for a light spice
flavor, definitely make this
cupcake. You'll be glad you
did. I like it topped with
Caramel Frosting or Cream
Cheese Icing.

Tip

Be sure to use unsweetened
applesauce in this recipe.

Variation

Add ½ cup (125 mL) raisins
to the batter.

- **Preheat oven to 350°F (180°C)**
- **Muffin pan, lined with paper liners**

1 cup	all-purpose flour	250 mL
¾ tsp	baking powder	3 mL
½ tsp	ground cinnamon	2 mL
¼ tsp	baking soda	1 mL
¼ tsp	ground ginger	1 mL
¼ tsp	ground allspice	1 mL
¼ tsp	ground nutmeg	1 mL
¼ tsp	salt	1 mL
¾ cup	granulated sugar	175 mL
¼ cup	unsalted butter, at room temperature	60 mL
1	egg	1
½ tsp	vanilla	2 mL
½ cup	unsweetened applesauce	125 mL
2 tbsp	buttermilk	30 mL
	Frosting (see Frosting suggestions, below)	

1. In a small bowl, whisk together flour, baking powder, cinnamon, baking soda, ginger, allspice, nutmeg and salt.

2. In a large bowl, using an electric mixer, beat together sugar and butter until well combined. Add egg, beating well. Mix in vanilla, beating until smooth. In a small bowl, whisk together applesauce and buttermilk.

3. Alternately beat flour mixture and buttermilk mixture into butter mixture, making three additions of flour mixture and two of buttermilk mixture, beating just until smooth.

4. Scoop batter into prepared pan. Bake in preheated oven for 20 to 25 minutes or until golden brown and tops of cupcakes spring back when lightly touched. Let cool in pan on rack for 10 minutes. Remove from pan and let cool completely on rack. Top cooled cupcakes with frosting.

> **Frosting suggestions:** Caramel Frosting (page 148), Cream Cheese Icing (page 158) or Maple Buttercream (page 167).

Chai Cupcakes

I love to add tea to my baked goods. This recipe is an adaptation of the Chocolate Chip Chai Cake in my first book, 125 Best Chocolate Chip Recipes. The original cake is so good that I felt obliged to make a cupcake version. These cupcakes are delicious with a pot of tea.

Tips

You can find chai tea bags in most grocery stores.

To substitute loose chai tea, grind it in a coffee or spice grinder until you have little bits (it doesn't have to be finely powdered). For one tea bag, substitute 1 tsp (5 mL) ground loose tea.

Variation

Add ½ cup (125 mL) white chocolate chips to the batter.

- **Preheat oven to 350°F (180°C)**
- **Muffin pan, lined with paper liners**

1 cup	all-purpose flour	250 mL
½ tsp	baking powder	2 mL
¼ tsp	baking soda	1 mL
¼ tsp	ground cardamom	1 mL
¼ tsp	ground allspice	1 mL
Pinch	salt	Pinch
1	chai spice tea bag (see Tips, left)	1
¾ cup	granulated sugar	175 mL
¼ cup	unsalted butter, at room temperature	60 mL
2	egg whites	2
½ tsp	vanilla	2 mL
⅔ cup	buttermilk	150 mL
	Frosting (see Frosting suggestions, below)	

1. In a bowl, whisk together flour, baking powder, baking soda, cardamom, allspice, salt and contents of tea bag.

2. In a large bowl, using an electric mixer, beat together sugar and butter until well combined. Add egg whites, one at a time, beating well after each addition. Mix in vanilla. Alternately beat in flour mixture and buttermilk, making three additions of flour mixture and two of buttermilk, beating until smooth.

3. Scoop batter into prepared pan. Bake in preheated oven for 20 to 25 minutes or until tops of cupcakes spring back when lightly touched. Let cool in pan on rack for 10 minutes. Remove from pan and let cool completely on rack. Top cooled cupcakes with frosting.

> **Frosting suggestions:** Caramel Frosting (page 148) or Cream Cheese Icing (page 158).

New Twists

Chocolate Chip Cookie Cupcakes 106

Raspberry Vanilla Cupcakes 107

Lamington Cupcakes 108

Chocolate Chip Cream Cheese Cupcakes 109

S'more Cupcakes 110

Cheesecake Cupcakes 112

Lemon Cheesecake Cupcakes 113

Chocolate Cheesecake Cupcakes 114

White Cupcakes with Coconut Frosting 116

Carrot Zucchini Cupcakes 117

Toasted Sesame Cupcakes 118

Sticky Date Cupcakes 119

Princess Cupcakes 120

Madeleine Cupcakes 121

Boston Cream Cupcakes 122

Orange-Scented Angel Food Cupcakes 124

Chocolate Chip Cookie Cupcakes

This recipe is adapted from the Quintessential Chocolate Chip Cookie recipe in my first book, 125 Best Chocolate Chip Recipes. *These cupcakes are soft, chewy and very delicious. They're a nice change from ordinary chocolate chip cookies.*

Tip

These cupcakes freeze well. Wrap them individually in plastic wrap and store them in resealable plastic freezer bags for up to 2 weeks.

Variation

Add ½ cup (125 mL) chopped macadamia nuts to the batter.

• **Preheat oven to 350°F (180°C)**
• **Muffin pan, lined with paper liners**

1½ cups	all-purpose flour	375 mL
½ tsp	baking powder	2 mL
Pinch	salt	Pinch
1¼ cups	packed light brown sugar	300 mL
½ cup	unsalted butter, at room temperature	125 mL
1 tsp	vanilla	5 mL
1	egg	1
1¼ cups	semisweet chocolate chips	300 mL
	Frosting (see Frosting suggestions, below)	

1. In a bowl, whisk together flour, baking powder and salt.

2. In a large bowl, using an electric mixer, beat together brown sugar and butter until well combined. Add vanilla, beating well. Add egg, beating well. Add flour mixture and beat just until combined. Stir in chocolate chips.

3. Scoop batter into prepared pan. Bake in preheated oven for 18 to 23 minutes or until cupcakes are puffed and golden (they will still be a little soft to the touch in the center and look somewhat undercooked). Let cool in pan on rack for 15 minutes or until cooled completely (so they don't crumble when removed). Remove from pan. Top cooled cupcakes with frosting.

> **Frosting suggestions:** Chocolate Fudge Frosting (page 149), Chocolate Glaze (page 150) or Vanilla Ice Cream (page 173) with a drizzle of Hot Fudge Sauce (page 163).

Raspberry Vanilla Cupcakes

Makes 12 cupcakes

These cupcakes are easy to prepare, reliable and always ready to please the pickiest palates. They're a great choice for afternoon tea, which is my favorite time to eat them.

Tip

These are best served the day that they're made.

Variation

Substitute apricot or cherry preserves for the raspberry.

- **Preheat oven to 350°F (180°C)**
- **Muffin pan, lined with paper liners**

1½ cups	all-purpose flour	375 mL
1½ tsp	baking powder	7 mL
¼ tsp	salt	1 mL
1 cup	granulated sugar	250 mL
½ cup	canola oil	125 mL
2	eggs	2
1 tsp	vanilla	5 mL
½ cup	milk	125 mL
⅓ cup	raspberry preserves	75 mL
	Frosting (see Frosting suggestions, below)	

1. In a small bowl, whisk together flour, baking powder and salt.

2. In a large bowl, whisk together sugar, oil, eggs and vanilla until smooth. Alternately whisk in flour mixture and milk, making three additions of flour mixture and two of milk, beating until smooth.

3. Scoop batter into prepared pan. Bake in preheated oven for 20 to 25 minutes or until golden brown and tops of cupcakes spring back when lightly touched. Let cool in pan on rack for 10 minutes. Remove from pan and let cool completely on rack.

4. Remove paper liners from cupcakes. Slice cupcakes in half horizontally. Spread bottoms with raspberry preserves, replacing tops. Top filled cupcakes with frosting.

> **Frosting suggestions:** Lemon Cream (page 164), Chocolate Glaze (page 150) or Cream Cheese Icing (page 158).

Lamington Cupcakes

Traditionally, Lamingtons are squares of cake coated in a chocolate glaze and rolled in coconut. This is my chocolate cupcake version, which is equally delicious.

Tips

To toast coconut: Place coconut in a nonstick skillet over medium heat and cook, stirring constantly, for 3 to 5 minutes or until lightly browned. Be careful not to let it burn. Transfer to a plate and let cool.

If you prefer a softer chocolate topping, serve immediately.

Variation

For a slightly different texture, don't toast the coconut before sprinkling it on cupcakes.

- **Preheat oven to 350°F (180°C)**
- **Muffin pan, lined with paper liners**

1¼ cups	all-purpose flour	300 mL
½ cup	loosely packed sweetened flaked coconut	125 mL
½ cup	unsweetened Dutch-process cocoa powder, sifted	125 mL
¾ tsp	baking soda	3 mL
¼ tsp	salt	1 mL
1 cup	granulated sugar	250 mL
⅓ cup	canola oil	75 mL
1	egg	1
1 tsp	vanilla	5 mL
¾ cup	buttermilk	175 mL
¾ cup	semisweet chocolate chips	175 mL
¼ cup	whipping (35%) cream	60 mL
½ cup	packed sweetened flaked coconut, lightly toasted and cooled (see Tips, left)	125 mL

1. In a small bowl, whisk together flour, coconut, cocoa powder, baking soda and salt.

2. In a bowl, whisk sugar, oil and egg until smooth. Add vanilla, mixing well. Alternately beat in flour mixture and buttermilk, making three additions of flour mixture and two of buttermilk, beating until smooth.

3. Scoop batter into prepared pan. Bake in preheated oven for 22 to 27 minutes or until tops spring back when lightly touched. Let cool in pan on rack for 10 minutes. Remove from pan and let cool completely on rack.

4. *Topping:* In a microwave-safe bowl, combine chocolate chips and cream. Microwave, uncovered, on High for 30 to 40 seconds or until cream is hot and chocolate is soft and almost melted. Stir mixture until smooth. Let stand for 5 minutes to cool slightly.

5. Working with one cupcake at a time, spread some of the chocolate mixture over top of cupcake. Sprinkle some of the toasted coconut over melted chocolate and place on a baking sheet. Repeat with remaining cupcakes, chocolate and coconut. Refrigerate cupcakes until chocolate is firm (see Tips, left).

Chocolate Chip Cream Cheese Cupcakes

These cupcakes are manna from heaven and very easy to make. The cream cheese filling is a surprise to the taste buds.

Tip

These cupcakes will only keep for 1 day. Make sure to refrigerate them until you're ready to serve them, because the cream cheese filling can spoil.

Variation

Omit the chocolate chips.

- **Preheat oven to 350°F (180°C)**
- **2 muffin pans (one 12-cup and one 6-cup), lined with paper liners**

1½ cups	all-purpose flour	375 mL
1½ tsp	baking powder	7 mL
¼ tsp	salt	1 mL
1 cup	granulated sugar	250 mL
½ cup	unsalted butter, melted and cooled slightly	125 mL
2	eggs	2
1 tsp	vanilla	5 mL
⅓ cup	milk	75 mL

Filling

8 oz	cream cheese, at room temperature	250 g
¼ cup	granulated sugar	60 mL
1	egg	1
1 cup	semisweet chocolate chips	250 mL
	Chocolate Fudge Frosting (see recipe, page 149)	

1. In a small bowl, whisk together flour, baking powder and salt.

2. In a large bowl, whisk together sugar, butter, eggs and vanilla until smooth. Alternately beat in flour mixture and milk, making three additions of flour mixture and two of milk, beating until smooth. Scoop batter into prepared pans, smoothing tops.

3. *Filling:* In a bowl, using an electric mixer, beat together cream cheese and sugar until smooth. Add egg, beating well. Stir in chocolate chips.

4. Top each cupcake with a scoop of cream cheese filling, smoothing top. Bake in preheated oven for 20 to 25 minutes or until cupcakes are puffed and golden, and cream cheese centers are just beginning to crack slightly and feel firm to the touch. Let cool in pan on rack for 10 minutes. Remove from pan and let cool completely on rack. Top cooled cupcakes with Chocolate Fudge Frosting.

S'more Cupcakes

Makes 12 cupcakes

When you think of camping in the great outdoors, what's the first thing that comes to mind? S'mores — everybody's favorite campfire treat. Now you can make them in your own kitchen. They taste so good you'll have everyone screaming, "S'mores, please!"

Tip

Although these cupcakes are best served the day that they're made, you can store them for 1 day, as long as they're covered and refrigerated.

- **Preheat oven to 350°F (180°C)**
- **Muffin pan, lined with paper liners**

1¼ cups	all-purpose flour	300 mL
½ cup	unsweetened Dutch-process cocoa powder, sifted	125 mL
¾ tsp	baking soda	3 mL
¼ tsp	salt	1 mL
1 cup	granulated sugar	250 mL
⅓ cup	canola oil	75 mL
1	egg	1
1 tsp	vanilla	5 mL
¾ cup	buttermilk	175 mL
½ cup	semisweet chocolate chips	125 mL

Filling
1 cup	marshmallow crème	250 mL

Glaze
½ cup	semisweet chocolate, chopped	125 mL
⅓ cup	whipping (35%) cream	75 mL

1. In a small bowl, whisk together flour, cocoa powder, baking soda and salt.

2. In a large bowl, whisk together sugar, oil, egg and vanilla until smooth. Alternately beat in flour mixture and buttermilk, making three additions of flour mixture and two of buttermilk, beating until smooth. Stir in chocolate chips.

3. Scoop batter into prepared pan. Bake in preheated oven for 22 to 27 minutes or until tops of cupcakes spring back when lightly touched. Let cool in pan on rack for 10 minutes. Remove from pan and let cool completely on rack. When cupcakes are completely cool, remove paper liners and slice cupcakes in half horizontally.

4. *Filling:* Working with one cupcake at a time, spread a layer of marshmallow crème on cut side of bottom half. Replace top half of cupcake, sandwiching the two halves together. Repeat with remaining cupcakes and marshmallow crème.

5. *Glaze:* In a microwave-safe bowl, combine chopped chocolate and cream. Microwave, uncovered, on High for 20 to 30 seconds or until cream is hot and chocolate is soft and almost melted. Stir until smooth. Let stand for 5 minutes to cool slightly.

6. Spread tops of cupcakes with chocolate glaze. Place cupcakes on a platter or baking sheet and refrigerate until glaze is firm.

Cheesecake Cupcakes

These miniature cheesecakes make star cupcakes! They're awesome and make a splash wherever you take and serve them.

Tip

Do not use paper liners for cheesecakes. Use only foil liners because the paper liners get soggy and the cheesecake will stick to them. The foil liners release the cheesecake cupcakes effortlessly.

Variations

Add ½ cup (125 mL) semisweet chocolate chips or chopped white chocolate to the batter for a chocolate chip version. Alternatively, spoon a dollop of cherry or berry pie filling over tops of cupcakes on top of sour cream topping.

- **Preheat oven to 350°F (180°C)**
- **Muffin pan, lined with foil liners (see Tip, left)**

Crust

¾ cup	graham cracker crumbs (about 7 graham crackers)	175 mL
3 tbsp	unsalted butter, melted	45 mL
1 tbsp	packed light brown sugar	15 mL

Filling

12 oz	cream cheese, at room temperature	375 g
½ cup	granulated sugar	125 mL
¼ cup	sour cream	60 mL
2	eggs	2

Topping

| ¾ cup | sour cream | 175 mL |
| 3 tbsp | granulated sugar | 45 mL |

1. *Crust:* In a small bowl, whisk together graham cracker crumbs, melted butter and brown sugar. Press crumb mixture into bottoms of prepared baking cups.

2. *Filling:* In a food processor fitted with a metal blade, pulse cream cheese until smooth. Add sugar, pulsing until smooth. Add sour cream and process until smooth. Add eggs, pulsing until smooth (you don't want to overprocess the mixture; you just want it to be smooth).

3. Scoop filling over crust in baking cups. Bake in preheated oven for 18 to 22 minutes or until centers of cupcakes are firm. Let cool in pan on rack for 5 minutes.

4. *Topping:* In a small bowl, stir together sour cream and sugar. Gently spoon and swirl (with back of spoon) sour cream mixture over cupcakes, covering tops. Return to oven and bake for 4 minutes. Let cupcakes cool to room temperature. Remove from pan and refrigerate for 2 hours or overnight to chill completely.

Lemon Cheesecake Cupcakes

Not only are these precious little cheesecakes beautiful, but they're also absolutely delicious! Lemon curd adds a big hit of fresh lemon flavor and is a perfect complement to the creamy cheesecake center.

Tip

You can freeze the baked and cooled cupcakes (without the lemon curd topping). Wrap them individually in plastic wrap and store them in resealable plastic freezer bags for up to 4 weeks. Once you have defrosted the cupcakes, top with the lemon curd.

Variation

Place a small dollop of whipped cream over the lemon curd before serving.

- **Preheat oven to 350°F (180°C)**
- **Muffin pan, lined with foil liners (see Tip, page 112)**

Crust

¾ cup	graham cracker crumbs (about 7 graham crackers)	175 mL
3 tbsp	unsalted butter, melted	45 mL
1 tbsp	packed light brown sugar	15 mL

Filling

12 oz	cream cheese, at room temperature	375 g
½ cup	granulated sugar	125 mL
¼ cup	sour cream	60 mL
2	eggs	2
1 tsp	grated lemon zest	5 mL
¾ cup	lemon curd, store-bought or homemade (see recipe, page 165)	175 mL

1. *Crust:* In a small bowl, whisk together graham cracker crumbs, melted butter and brown sugar. Press crumb mixture into bottoms of prepared baking cups.

2. *Filling:* In a food processor fitted with a metal blade, pulse cream cheese until smooth. Add sugar, pulsing until smooth. Add sour cream and process until smooth. Add eggs and lemon zest, pulsing until smooth (you don't want to overprocess the mixture; you just want it to be smooth).

3. Scoop filling over crust in baking cups. Bake in preheated oven for 18 to 22 minutes or until the centers of cupcakes are firm. Let cool in pan on rack for 10 minutes. Remove from pan and refrigerate for 2 hours or overnight. Before serving, place a dollop of lemon curd over top of each cupcake and swirl lightly with back of spoon.

Chocolate Cheesecake Cupcakes

Makes 12 cupcakes

Cheesecake does not get any easier than this. Instead of a traditional crust, simply place a whole chocolate sandwich cookie in the bottom of the baking cup, then top it with a blend of cream cheese and melted chocolate. This is definitely a to-die-for dessert.

Tips

Make sure not to overprocess the cheesecake filling.

These cupcakes freeze well. Wrap them individually in plastic wrap and store them in resealable plastic freezer bags for up to 3 weeks.

- **Preheat oven to 350°F (180°C)**
- **Muffin pan, lined with foil liners (see Tip, page 112)**

12	chocolate sandwich cookies	12
3 oz	bittersweet or semisweet chocolate, chopped	90 g
1 oz	unsweetened chocolate, chopped	30 g
12 oz	cream cheese, at room temperature	375 g
½ cup	granulated sugar	125 mL
¼ cup	sour cream	60 mL
2 tbsp	chocolate cream liqueur	30 mL
2	eggs	2

Topping

¾ cup	sour cream	175 mL
3 tbsp	granulated sugar	45 mL
1 tbsp	chocolate cream liqueur	15 mL
	Unsweetened Dutch-process cocoa powder, sifted	

1. Place one chocolate sandwich cookie in bottom of each foil-lined cup and set aside.

2. In a microwave-safe bowl, combine bittersweet and unsweetened chocolates. Microwave, uncovered, on High for 45 to 50 seconds, stirring after 30 seconds, or until chocolate is soft and almost melted. Stir until smooth. Set aside and let cool slightly.

3. In a food processor fitted with a metal blade, pulse cream cheese until smooth. Add sugar, pulsing until smooth. Add melted chocolate and process until smooth. Add sour cream and liqueur, blending well. Add eggs, pulsing just until smooth (you don't want to overprocess the mixture; you just want it to be smooth).

Variations

Omit sour cream topping. Just before serving, whip together ¾ cup (175 mL) whipping (35%) cream, 2 tbsp (30 mL) confectioner's sugar and ½ tsp (2 mL) vanilla. Spread or dollop whipped cream mixture over tops of cupcakes. Sprinkle grated chocolate over whipped cream and serve.

You can use crème de cacao in place of chocolate liqueur.

4. Scoop batter into cookie-lined cups. Bake in preheated oven for 18 to 22 minutes or until centers of cupcakes are firm. Let cool in pan on rack for 5 minutes.

5. *Topping:* In a small bowl, stir together sour cream, sugar and liqueur. Gently spoon and swirl (with back of spoon) sour cream mixture over cupcakes, covering tops. Return to oven and bake for 4 minutes. Let cupcakes cool in pan on rack to room temperature. Cover and refrigerate for 2 hours or overnight to chill completely. Just before serving, lightly dust tops of cupcakes with cocoa powder.

White Cupcakes with Coconut Frosting

Makes 12 cupcakes

My sister-in-law Randie felt it was important to include a white cupcake with coconut frosting. So I immediately got to work developing a coconut cupcake worthy of a fancy dinner party. Randie, this cupcake recipe is for you.

Tip

When making the frosting for these cupcakes, I added 1 tsp (5 mL) coconut rum to the Cream Cheese Icing.

Variation

Substitute light-color rum for the coconut rum. You can also substitute Easy Buttercream Frosting (page 159) for the Cream Cheese Icing.

- **Preheat oven to 350°F (180°C)**
- **Muffin pan, lined with paper liners**

1½ cups	all-purpose flour	375 mL
1½ tsp	baking powder	7 mL
¼ tsp	salt	1 mL
1 cup	granulated sugar	250 mL
½ cup	unsalted butter, melted and cooled slightly	125 mL
2	eggs	2
2 tbsp	coconut rum	30 mL
½ tsp	vanilla	2 mL
⅔ cup	milk	150 mL
	Cream Cheese Icing (see recipe, page 158)	
½ cup	loosely packed sweetened flaked coconut	125 mL

1. In a small bowl, whisk together flour, baking powder and salt.

2. In a large bowl, whisk together sugar, butter, eggs, rum and vanilla until smooth. Alternately whisk in flour mixture and milk, making three additions of flour mixture and two of milk, beating just until smooth.

3. Scoop batter into prepared pan. Bake in preheated oven for 20 to 25 minutes or until golden brown and tops of cupcakes spring back when lightly touched. Let cool in pan on rack for 10 minutes. Remove from pan and let cool completely on rack.

4. Spread Cream Cheese Icing over cooled cupcakes. Sprinkle coconut over frosting.

Carrot Zucchini Cupcakes

I can't emphasize enough the delight I receive making desserts with certain vegetables. They always turn out moist, tender and delicious.

Tips

It is best to use a spoon or spatula to stir the carrot and zucchini together with the flour mixture rather than a whisk because the vegetables tend to get gummed up in the whisk.

Be sure to use nice crisp vegetables for this recipe because they will shred well.

Variation

Add $\frac{1}{3}$ cup (75 mL) loosely packed sweetened flaked coconut to the batter.

- **Preheat oven to 350°F (180°C)**
- **Muffin pan, lined with paper liners**

1½ cups	all-purpose flour	375 mL
1½ tsp	baking powder	7 mL
½ tsp	ground cinnamon	2 mL
¼ tsp	salt	1 mL
1 cup	granulated sugar	250 mL
½ cup	unsalted butter, melted and cooled slightly	125 mL
2	eggs	2
1 cup	shredded carrot (about 1 large carrot)	250 mL
1 cup	shredded zucchini (about 1 small zucchini)	250 mL
⅓ cup	milk	75 mL
	Frosting (see Frosting suggestions, below)	

1. In a small bowl, whisk together flour, baking powder, cinnamon and salt.

2. In a large bowl, whisk together sugar, butter and eggs until smooth. Add shredded carrot and zucchini, beating until mixed. Alternately stir in flour mixture and milk, making three additions of flour mixture and two of milk, beating until smooth (see Tips, left).

3. Scoop batter into prepared pan. Bake in preheated oven for 20 to 25 minutes or until golden brown and tops of cupcakes spring back when lightly touched. Let cool in pan on rack for 10 minutes. Remove from pan and let cool completely on rack. Top cooled cupcakes with frosting.

> **Frosting suggestions:** Cream Cheese Icing (page 158), Orange Cream Cheese Icing (page 168) or Caramel Frosting (page 148).

Toasted Sesame Cupcakes

Makes 12 cupcakes

This cupcake has an incredibly rich flavor from the toasted sesame seeds. It makes a perfect ending for an Asian or Mediterranean meal.

Tip

To toast sesame seeds: Heat a small nonstick skillet over medium heat. Add sesame seeds and cook, stirring or shaking skillet continuously, for 3 minutes or until seeds start to darken and look toasted. Transfer seeds to a plate and let cool.

Variation

Add ½ cup (125 mL) white chocolate chips or coarsely chopped white chocolate to the batter.

- **Preheat oven to 350°F (180°C)**
- **Muffin pan, lined with paper liners**

1 cup	all-purpose flour	250 mL
¼ cup	sesame seeds, toasted (see Tip, left)	60 mL
½ tsp	baking powder	2 mL
¼ tsp	baking soda	1 mL
Pinch	salt	Pinch
¾ cup	granulated sugar	175 mL
¼ cup	unsalted butter, at room temperature	60 mL
2	egg whites	2
⅔ cup	buttermilk	150 mL
	Easy Buttercream Frosting (see recipe, page 159)	

1. In a small bowl, whisk together flour, sesame seeds, baking powder, baking soda and salt.

2. In a bowl, using an electric mixer, beat together sugar and butter until well combined. Add egg whites, one at a time, beating well after each addition. Alternately beat in flour mixture and buttermilk, making three additions of flour mixture and two of buttermilk, beating until smooth.

3. Scoop batter into prepared pan. Bake in preheated oven for 20 to 25 minutes or until tops of cupcakes spring back when lightly touched. Let cool in pan on rack for 10 minutes. Remove from pan and let cool completely on rack. Top cooled cupcakes with Easy Buttercream Frosting.

Sticky Date Cupcakes

Makes 12 cupcakes

When I was in London several years ago, I fell in love with sticky date pudding cakes. I promised myself that I would include a version in one of my cookbooks. Baking these divine cakes in a cupcake pan turned out to be a natural. Make sure to top the warm cupcakes with warm Chocolate Toffee Sauce for a killer dessert.

Tip

You can make these cupcakes up to 1 week ahead. Wrap them individually in plastic wrap and freeze them in resealable plastic freezer bags. Thaw, warm slightly and serve with hot Chocolate Toffee Sauce.

Variation

Add 1/3 cup (75 mL) finely chopped semisweet chocolate to the batter.

- **Preheat oven to 350°F (180°C)**
- **Muffin pan, lined with paper liners**

1 1/3 cups	pitted dates (7 oz/210 g), chopped	325 mL
1/3 cup	water	75 mL
1 1/2 cups	all-purpose flour	375 mL
1 1/2 tsp	baking powder	7 mL
1/4 tsp	salt	1 mL
1/2 cup	granulated sugar	125 mL
1/3 cup	packed brown sugar	75 mL
1/2 cup	unsalted butter, at room temperature	125 mL
2	eggs	2
1/4 cup	milk	60 mL
	Chocolate Toffee Sauce (see recipe, page 153)	

1. In a small saucepan over medium heat, combine dates and water. Cook until dates are soft and water is absorbed. Set aside and let cool.

2. In a small bowl, whisk together flour, baking powder and salt.

3. In a large bowl, using an electric mixer, beat together granulated and brown sugars and butter until well combined. Add eggs, one at a time, beating well after each addition. Add flour mixture, beating until combined. Add milk and reserved date mixture, beating until smooth.

4. Scoop batter into prepared pan. Bake in preheated oven for 20 to 25 minutes or until golden brown and tops of cupcakes spring back when lightly touched. Let cool in pan on rack for 10 minutes. Remove from pan and let cool completely on rack.

5. Remove paper liners from cupcakes. Top warm cupcakes with Chocolate Toffee Sauce.

Princess Cupcakes

Makes 12 cupcakes

I picture tea parties and miniature tea sets when I taste these cupcakes. They're both elegant and delicious, definitely worthy of an afternoon tea party shared with royalty.

Tip

You can make and fill the cupcakes early in the day and frost them right before serving.

Variation

Substitute raspberry preserves for the apricot.

- **Preheat oven to 350°F (180°C)**
- **Muffin pan, lined with paper liners**

1½ cups	all-purpose flour	375 mL
¾ tsp	baking powder	3 mL
½ tsp	baking soda	2 mL
¼ tsp	salt	1 mL
1¼ cups	granulated sugar	300 mL
6 tbsp	unsalted butter, at room temperature	90 mL
3	egg whites	3
1 tsp	vanilla	5 mL
1 cup	buttermilk	250 mL
¼ cup	apricot preserves	60 mL
1	tube (7 oz/210 g) marzipan	1
	Frosting (see Frosting suggestions, below)	

1. In a small bowl, whisk together flour, baking powder, baking soda and salt.

2. In a bowl, using an electric mixer, beat together sugar and butter until well combined. Add egg whites, one at a time, beating well after each addition. Beat in vanilla. Alternately beat in flour mixture and buttermilk, making three additions of flour mixture and two of buttermilk, beating until smooth.

3. Scoop batter into prepared pan. Bake in preheated oven for 22 to 27 minutes or until tops of cupcakes spring back when lightly touched. Let cool in pan on rack for 10 minutes. Remove from pan and let cool completely on rack.

4. Remove paper liners from cooled cupcakes. Slice cupcakes in half horizontally. On bottom halves, spread apricot preserves. Slice marzipan into 12 pieces and lightly press each into a 2-inch (5 cm) disc. Place discs on top of apricot jam and replace tops. Let cupcakes sit for about 30 minutes to firm up before frosting.

> **Frosting suggestions:** Easy Buttercream Frosting (page 159) or Whipped Cream Topping (page 175).

Madeleine Cupcakes

I love madeleines, the French shell-shaped cakey cookies that Marcel Proust made so famous. My husband, Jay, suggested that I try making my madeleine batter into cupcakes. Well, lo and behold, we've got a new classic here.

Tip

For cupcakes in a hurry, keep a batch of these delectable cupcakes, unfrosted, in your freezer. When thawed, simply dust with confectioner's sugar or top with your frosting of choice.

Variation

For a lemon version, omit the vanilla, almond extract and orange zest. Add 1 tbsp (15 mL) grated lemon zest and 1 tsp (5 mL) lemon oil or lemon extract (see Tip, page 35).

- • **Preheat oven to 350°F (180°C)**
- • **Muffin pan, lined with paper liners**

2¼ cups	confectioner's (icing) sugar, sifted	550 mL
1 cup	unsalted butter, at room temperature	250 mL
4	eggs	4
1 tbsp	finely grated orange zest	15 mL
½ tsp	vanilla	2 mL
½ tsp	almond extract	2 mL
1⅔ cups	all-purpose flour	400 mL
¼ tsp	salt	1 mL
	Frosting (see Frosting suggestions, below)	

1. In a bowl, using an electric mixer, beat together sugar and butter until well combined (this might take a few minutes). Add eggs, one at a time, beating well after each addition. Add orange zest, vanilla and almond extract. Add flour and salt, beating until smooth.

2. Scoop batter into prepared pan. Bake in preheated oven for 20 to 25 minutes or until tops of cupcakes spring back when lightly touched. Let cool in pan on rack for 10 minutes. Remove from pan and let cool completely on rack. Top cooled cupcakes with frosting.

> **Frosting suggestions:** Chocolate Fudge Frosting (page 149), Orange Cream Cheese Icing (page 168) or Easy Buttercream Frosting (page 159).

Boston Cream Cupcakes

Though this recipe may look complicated, it's really very easy. You can serve these cupcakes as a centerpiece dessert for a casual get-together, and I guarantee they will create a lot of oohs and aahs. To make assembly speedier, you can prepare the custard a day ahead. Then simply make the glaze and assemble the cakes the day of the party.

Tip

You can store these cupcakes, refrigerated and well-wrapped, for up to 1 day.

Variation

For an all-vanilla version, omit the chocolate glaze. Top with Vanilla Cream Frosting (page 160) or Easy Buttercream Frosting (page 159).

- **Preheat oven to 350°F (180°C)**
- **Muffin pan, lined with paper liners**

1½ cups	all-purpose flour	375 mL
1½ tsp	baking powder	7 mL
¼ tsp	salt	1 mL
1 cup	granulated sugar	250 mL
½ cup	unsalted butter, melted and cooled slightly	125 mL
2	eggs	2
½ tsp	vanilla	2 mL
½ cup	milk	125 mL

Filling

3 tbsp	granulated sugar	45 mL
2 tbsp	cornstarch	30 mL
Pinch	salt	Pinch
2	egg yolks	2
½ cup	milk	125 mL
¼ cup + 3 tbsp	whipping (35%) cream, divided	60 mL + 45 mL
2 tsp	unsalted butter	10 mL
½ tsp	vanilla paste or vanilla (see Tip, page 28)	2 mL

Glaze

½ cup	semisweet chocolate, chopped	125 mL
⅓ cup	whipping (35%) cream	75 mL

1. In a small bowl, whisk together flour, baking powder and salt.

2. In a large bowl, whisk together sugar, butter, eggs and vanilla until smooth. Alternately whisk in flour mixture and milk, making three additions of flour mixture and two of milk, beating until smooth.

3. Scoop batter into prepared pan. Bake in preheated oven for 20 to 25 minutes or until golden brown and tops of cupcakes spring back when lightly touched. Let cool in pan on rack for 10 minutes. Remove from pan and let cool completely on rack.

4. *Filling:* In a heavy saucepan, whisk together sugar, cornstarch and salt. Whisk in egg yolks, milk and $\frac{1}{4}$ cup (60 mL) cream until smooth. Bring mixture to a simmer over medium heat, whisking continuously. Once mixture is at a simmer and begins to thicken, remove from heat but continue whisking until very thick. Whisk in butter and vanilla paste until butter is melted and custard is smooth.

5. Spoon custard into a small bowl. Fill a slightly larger bowl with ice. Place small bowl of custard on top of ice. Whisk custard until cool. Remove small bowl, dry bottom and sides with a towel so that no moisture gets inside bowl. Whisk in remaining 3 tbsp (45 mL) whipping cream. Place a piece of plastic wrap on surface of custard and refrigerate for 40 minutes or until chilled, or for up to 2 days.

6. When cupcakes are cool, peel off paper liners. Carefully slice tops off cupcakes. Using a small spoon, scoop out about a rounded teaspoonful (5 mL) of cake from bottom half (being careful not to scoop a hole in bottom). Spread a layer of reserved cooled custard on cut side of bottom half (filling small hole with custard, too). Replace tops of cupcakes over custard, sandwiching two halves together. Repeat with remaining cupcakes and custard.

7. *Glaze:* In a microwave-safe bowl, combine chocolate and cream. Microwave, uncovered, on High for 40 seconds or until cream is hot and chocolate is soft and almost melted. Stir until smooth. Let chocolate mixture sit for 5 minutes or until slightly cooled but still spreadable.

8. Spread tops of cupcakes with chocolate glaze. Place cupcakes on a platter or baking sheet and refrigerate until ready to serve. These cupcakes need to stay refrigerated so that the custard filling doesn't spoil. They can be served straight from the refrigerator or set out at room temperature for about 15 minutes before serving to remove the chill.

Orange-Scented Angel Food Cupcakes

This is a deliciously virtuous cupcake that's made from a light-as-air egg white batter with no added butter or oil. I adapted the cupcakes from a recipe by Melanie Barnard in Cooking Light Magazine. It's one heavenly cupcake!

Tip

Eggs separate best when they're cold. Once separated, let the whites come to room temperature before beating.

- **Preheat oven to 325°F (160°C)**
- **Muffin pan, lined with foil liners**

²⁄₃ cup	granulated sugar, divided	150 mL
¹⁄₂ cup	cake flour, sifted	125 mL
6	egg whites, at room temperature (see Tip, left)	6
¹⁄₄ tsp	cream of tartar	1 mL
Pinch	salt	Pinch
1 tbsp	grated orange zest	15 mL
2 tsp	freshly squeezed orange juice	10 mL
1 tsp	vanilla	5 mL
¹⁄₂ cup	semisweet chocolate chips	125 mL

1. In a small bowl, whisk together ¹⁄₃ cup (75 mL) of the sugar and the flour.

2. In a large bowl, using a stand mixer with the whisk attachment, on high speed, beat egg whites until foamy. Add cream of tartar and salt, whipping until soft peaks form. Add remaining sugar, 2 tbsp (30 mL) at a time, beating until stiff peaks form. Beat in orange zest and juice, and vanilla.

3. Sift one-third of flour mixture over egg white mixture and fold in gently. Repeat two more times with remaining flour mixture until flour mixture is incorporated. Fold in chocolate chips.

4. Scoop batter into prepared pan. Bake in preheated oven for 19 minutes or until tops of cupcakes spring back when lightly touched. Let cool in pan on rack for 10 minutes. Remove from pan and let cool completely on rack. Cupcakes will shrink as they cool.

Vegan

Vegan Chocolate Cherry Cupcakes 126

Vegan Chocolate Cinnamon Cupcakes 127

Vegan Almond Cupcakes 128

Vegan Carrot Raisin Cupcakes 129

Vegan Cherry Almond Cupcakes 130

Vegan Chocolate Cupcakes 131

Vegan Chocolate Orange Cupcakes 132

Vegan Chocolate Peppermint Cupcakes 134

Vegan Chocolate Raspberry Cupcakes 135

Vegan Cinnamon Almond Cupcakes 136

Vegan Coconut Cupcakes 137

Vegan Coffee Cupcakes 138

Vegan Creamsicle Cupcakes 139

Vegan Green Tea Matcha Cupcakes 140

Vegan Lemon Cupcakes 141

Vegan Mocha Cupcakes 142

Vegan Oat Spice Cupcakes 143

Vegan Pumpkin Pecan Cupcakes 144

Vegan Sweet Vanilla Cupcakes 145

Vegan Toasted Sesame Cupcakes 146

Vegan Chocolate Cherry Cupcakes

Too busy to cook? This quick and easy recipe can entice the weary out of the chair and into the kitchen. I've said it before and I'll say it again: chocolate and cherry is the winningest combo of them all.

Tip

These cupcakes are best frosted and served the day that they're made.

Variation

Add ½ cup (125 mL) dairy-free semisweet chocolate chips along with the vinegar.

- **Preheat oven to 350°F (180°C)**
- **Muffin pan, lined with paper liners**

1½ cups	all-purpose flour	375 mL
½ cup	unsweetened Dutch-process cocoa powder, sifted	125 mL
½ tsp	baking soda	2 mL
Pinch	salt	Pinch
1 cup	granulated sugar	250 mL
½ cup	canola oil	125 mL
1 cup	canned cherry pie filling (not canned cherries in juice)	250 mL
½ tsp	vanilla	2 mL
½ tsp	almond extract	2 mL
⅓ cup	cherry juice or cranberry juice cocktail	75 mL
2 tbsp	balsamic vinegar	30 mL
	Vegan Chocolate Fudge Frosting (see recipe, page 177)	

1. In a small bowl, whisk together flour, cocoa powder, baking soda and salt.

2. In a large bowl, whisk together sugar and oil. Mix in cherry pie filling, vanilla and almond extract. Alternately whisk in flour mixture and cherry juice, making three additions of flour mixture and two of juice, beating until batter is smooth. Mix in vinegar.

3. Scoop batter into prepared pan. Bake in preheated oven for 22 to 25 minutes or until tops of cupcakes spring back when lightly touched. Let cool in pan on rack for 10 minutes. Remove from pan and let cool completely on rack. Top cooled cupcakes with frosting.

Vegan Chocolate Cinnamon Cupcakes

Mexican chocolate — a blend of chocolate, almond and cinnamon flavors — is usually served hot, blended with milk. I took the delicious flavors of Mexican chocolate and added them to this delectable cupcake. Viva el chocolate!

Tip

Although it might seem weird to add the balsamic vinegar to the batter, it reacts with the baking soda to make the cupcakes rise (since there are no eggs in the batter). The vinegar evaporates while baking, so there is no vinegary taste.

- **Preheat oven to 350°F (180°C)**
- **Muffin pan, lined with paper liners**

1½ cups	all-purpose flour	375 mL
½ cup	unsweetened Dutch-process cocoa powder, sifted	125 mL
½ tsp	ground cinnamon	2 mL
½ tsp	baking soda	2 mL
Pinch	salt	Pinch
1¼ cups	granulated sugar	300 mL
¾ cup	strong brewed coffee, at room temperature	175 mL
½ cup	canola oil	125 mL
1 tsp	vanilla	5 mL
½ tsp	almond extract	2 mL
2 tbsp	balsamic vinegar	30 mL
½ cup	dairy-free semisweet chocolate chips	125 mL
	Vegan Chocolate Fudge Frosting (see recipe, page 177)	

1. In a small bowl, whisk together flour, cocoa powder, cinnamon, baking soda and salt.

2. In a large bowl, whisk together sugar, coffee, oil, vanilla and almond extract. Add flour mixture, beating until smooth. Mix in balsamic vinegar. Stir in chocolate chips.

3. Scoop batter into prepared pan. Bake in preheated oven for 25 minutes or until tops of cupcakes spring back when lightly touched. Let cool in pan on rack for 10 minutes. Remove from pan and let cool completely on rack. Top cooled cupcakes with frosting.

Vegan Almond Cupcakes

These are one of my favorite cupcakes, full of delicious almond flavor. You can also have a lot of fun with it, since it's a great basic cupcake open to all sorts of flavored frostings.

Tip

Make sure to divide the batter evenly among the muffin cups. If you wind up with a little more batter, depending on the size of your pan, you can always bake up an additional cupcake or two.

Variation

Add 2 to 3 tbsp (30 to 45 mL) poppy seeds to the batter for an almond poppy seed variation.

- **Preheat oven to 350°F (180°C)**
- **Muffin pan, lined with paper liners**

1 cup	soy milk	250 mL
1 tsp	apple cider vinegar	5 mL
1½ cups	all-purpose flour	375 mL
¼ cup	potato starch	60 mL
2 tsp	baking powder	10 mL
¼ tsp	salt	1 mL
1 cup + 2 tbsp	granulated sugar	280 mL
½ cup	canola oil	125 mL
1 tbsp	almond extract	15 mL
	Frosting (see Frosting suggestions, below)	

1. In a small bowl, whisk together soy milk and vinegar. Set aside.

2. In another bowl, whisk together flour, potato starch, baking powder and salt.

3. In a large bowl, whisk together half of the soy milk mixture, sugar, oil and almond extract. Add half of the flour mixture, whisking just until incorporated. Add remaining soy milk and flour mixtures, whisking just until smooth.

4. Scoop batter into prepared pan, making sure not to fill the cups more than ⅔ of the way as they will overflow. Bake in preheated oven for 25 to 35 minutes or until tops of cupcakes spring back when lightly touched. Let cool in pan on rack for 10 minutes. Carefully remove from pan and let cool completely on rack. Top cooled cupcakes with frosting.

> **Frosting suggestions:** Vegan Fluffy Almond Cream Frosting (page 178), Vegan Fluffy Vanilla Cream Frosting (page 183) or Vegan Chocolate Fudge Frosting (page 177).

Vegan Carrot Raisin Cupcakes

Makes 12 cupcakes

If you are a carrot cake lover, then this is your cupcake. It has a light spiced flavor, which pairs well with the carrots and raisins.

Tip

Even though you may be tempted, don't try to fit all of the batter into 12 cupcakes because the cupcakes will spill over in your pan.

Variation

Substitute ½ cup (125 mL) chopped walnuts or pecans for the raisins, or omit them all together.

- Preheat oven to 350°F (180°C)
- Muffin pan, lined with paper liners

1 cup	soy milk	250 mL
1 tsp	apple cider vinegar	5 mL
1½ cups	all-purpose flour	375 mL
¼ cup	potato starch	60 mL
2 tsp	baking powder	10 mL
1½ tsp	ground cinnamon	7 mL
½ tsp	ground allspice	2 mL
¼ tsp	salt	1 mL
1 cup + 2 tbsp	granulated sugar	280 mL
½ cup	canola oil	125 mL
1 cup	shredded carrots (not packed)	250 mL
½ cup	raisins	125 mL
	Frosting (see Frosting suggestions, below)	

1. In a small bowl, whisk together soy milk and vinegar. Set aside.

2. In another bowl, whisk together flour, potato starch, baking powder, cinnamon, allspice and salt.

3. In a large bowl, whisk together half of the soy milk mixture, sugar and oil. Add half of the flour mixture, whisking just until incorporated. Add remaining soy milk and flour mixtures, carrots and raisins, stirring just until smooth.

4. Scoop batter into prepared pan, making sure not to fill the cups more than ⅔ of the way as they will overflow. Bake in preheated oven for 25 to 35 minutes or until tops of cupcakes spring back when lightly touched. Let cool in pan on rack for 10 minutes. Carefully remove from pan and let cool completely on rack. Top cooled cupcakes with frosting.

> **Frosting suggestions:** Vegan Cream Cheese Frosting (page 184) or Vegan Fluffy Vanilla Cream Frosting (page 183).

Vegan Cherry Almond Cupcakes

These cupcakes were inspired by a cherry almond pound cake I used to make. The almond flavor complements the cherries that make the cake a gorgeous light pink color.

Tip

Look for the canned cherry pie filling in your local grocery store.

Variation

Sprinkle a few dairy-free chocolate chips into each cupcake before baking for a chocolate cherry almond version.

- **Preheat oven to 350°F (180°C)**
- **Muffin pan, lined with paper liners**

1½ cups	all-purpose flour	375 mL
¼ cup	potato starch	60 mL
2 tsp	baking powder	10 mL
¼ tsp	salt	1 mL
1 cup	canned cherry pie filling (see Tip, left)	250 mL
¾ cup + 2 tbsp	granulated sugar	200 mL
½ cup	canola oil	125 mL
1½ tsp	almond extract	7 mL
¼ cup	soy milk	60 mL
	Frosting (see Frosting suggestions, below)	

1. In a small bowl, whisk together flour, potato starch, baking powder and salt.

2. In a large bowl, stir together cherry pie filling, sugar, oil and almond extract. Don't worry if the cherries get a little smashed. Add half of the flour mixture, stirring just until incorporated. Add soy milk and remaining flour, stirring just until smooth.

3. Scoop batter into prepared pan, making sure not to fill the cups more than ⅔ of the way as they will overflow. Bake in preheated oven for 25 to 35 minutes or until tops of cupcakes spring back when lightly touched. Let cool in pan on rack for 10 minutes. Carefully remove from pan and let cool completely on rack. Top cooled cupcakes with frosting.

> **Frosting suggestions:** Vegan Fluffy Vanilla Cream Frosting (page 183), Vegan Chocolate Fudge Frosting (page 177) or Vegan Fluffy Almond Cream Frosting (page 178).

Vegan Chocolate Cupcakes

I think of this recipe as the little black dress. These cupcakes go with everything, but are stylish enough for even the fanciest of events.

Tip

You can also make these cupcakes and freeze them ahead in a resealable bag.

Variations

Stir ⅓ cup (75 mL) chopped dried pitted cherries into the batter for a chocolate cherry version.

These cupcakes are delicious filled with raspberry jam. Simply remove the wrappers, slice in half horizontally and spread a dollop of raspberry jam. Replace tops, place in a fresh cupcake wrapper and frost as usual.

- **Preheat oven to 350°F (180°C)**
- **Muffin pan, lined with paper liners**

1 cup	plain or vanilla soy milk	250 mL
1 tsp	apple cider vinegar	5 mL
1 cup	all-purpose flour	250 mL
½ cup	unsweetened Dutch-process cocoa powder, sifted	125 mL
¼ cup	potato starch	60 mL
2 tsp	baking powder	10 mL
¼ tsp	salt	1 mL
1 cup + 2 tbsp	granulated sugar	280 mL
½ cup	canola oil	125 mL
1 tbsp	vanilla	15 mL
	Frosting (see Frosting suggestions, below)	

1. In a small bowl, whisk together soy milk and vinegar. Set aside.

2. In another bowl, whisk together flour, cocoa powder, potato starch, baking powder and salt.

3. In a large bowl, whisk together half of the soy milk mixture, sugar, oil and vanilla. Add half of the flour mixture, whisking just until incorporated. Add remaining soy milk and flour mixtures, whisking just until smooth.

4. Scoop batter into prepared pan, making sure not to fill the cups more than ⅔ of the way as they will overflow. Bake for 25 to 35 minutes or until tops of cupcakes spring back when lightly touched. Let cool in pan on rack for 10 minutes. Carefully remove from pan and let cool completely on rack. Top cooled cupcakes with frosting.

> **Frosting suggestions:** Vegan Peanut Butter Frosting (page 182), Vegan Chocolate Fudge Frosting (page 177), Vegan Cream Cheese Frosting (page 184), Vegan Fluffy Almond Cream Frosting (page 178) or Vegan Fluffy Vanilla Cream Frosting (page 183).

Vegan Chocolate Orange Cupcakes

When I was young, I adored the chocolate orange candy that looked just like an orange, wrapped up in pretty blue foil. The taste was a delicious mix of chocolate and orange and the candy would even fall apart into slices. Well, that's the flavor of these special cupcakes, which I can't get enough of.

Tip

The chocolate chips are optional here. They give the cupcakes another shot of chocolate. The tops of cupcakes might sink in a little, though nothing that a little chocolate frosting wouldn't cover.

- **Preheat oven to 350°F (180°C)**
- **Muffin pan, lined with paper liners**

¾ cup	soy milk	175 mL
1 tsp	apple cider vinegar	5 mL
1 cup	all-purpose flour	250 mL
½ cup	unsweetened Dutch-process cocoa powder, sifted	125 mL
¼ cup	potato starch	60 mL
2 tsp	baking powder	10 mL
¼ tsp	salt	1 mL
1 cup + 2 tbsp	granulated sugar	280 mL
½ cup	canola oil	125 mL
2 tbsp	frozen orange juice concentrate, thawed	30 mL
1 tbsp	finely grated tangerine or orange zest	15 mL
1 tbsp	vanilla	15 mL
½ tsp	pure orange oil	2 mL
⅓ cup	dairy-free semisweet chocolate chips, optional	75 mL
	Frosting (see Frosting suggestions, right)	

1. In a small bowl, whisk together soy milk and vinegar. Set aside.

2. In another bowl, whisk together flour, cocoa powder, potato starch, baking powder and salt.

3. In a large bowl, whisk together half of the soy milk mixture, sugar, canola oil, orange juice, orange zest, vanilla and orange oil. Add half of the flour mixture, whisking just until incorporated. Add remaining soy milk and flour mixtures, whisking just until smooth.

4. Scoop batter into prepared pan, making sure not to fill the cups more than $\frac{2}{3}$ of the way as they will overflow. Sprinkle about 4 to 6 chocolate chips, if using, on top of each cupcake. Lightly press them into the batter, making sure that there isn't a dent on the top. Bake for 25 to 35 minutes or until tops of cupcakes spring back when lightly touched. Let cool in pan on rack for 10 minutes. Carefully remove from pan and let cool completely on rack. Top cooled cupcakes with frosting.

Frosting suggestions: Vegan Cream Cheese Frosting (page 184) or Vegan Chocolate Fudge Frosting (page 177).

Vegan Chocolate Peppermint Cupcakes

I love chocolate and mint together, which is why I think these cupcakes are tops. You can top these lovely cakes with Vegan Chocolate Fudge Frosting, which takes them into a whole other realm.

Tip

It's fun to decorate the frosted tops of these cupcakes with crushed peppermint candies or candy canes.

- **Preheat oven to 350°F (180°C)**
- **Muffin pan, lined with paper liners**

³⁄₄ cup	soy milk	175 mL
1 tsp	apple cider vinegar	5 mL
1 cup	all-purpose flour	250 mL
¹⁄₂ cup	unsweetened Dutch-process cocoa powder, sifted	125 mL
¹⁄₄ cup	potato starch	60 mL
2 tsp	baking powder	10 mL
¹⁄₄ tsp	salt	1 mL
1¹⁄₄ cups	granulated sugar	300 mL
¹⁄₂ cup	canola oil	125 mL
1 tsp	pure peppermint extract	5 mL
	Frosting (see Frosting suggestions, below)	

1. In a small bowl, whisk together soy milk and vinegar. Set aside.

2. In another bowl, whisk together flour, cocoa powder, potato starch, baking powder and salt.

3. In a large bowl, whisk together sugar, oil and peppermint extract. Add half of the soy milk mixture, whisking until smooth. Add half of the flour mixture, whisking just until incorporated. Add remaining soy milk and flour mixtures, whisking just until smooth.

4. Scoop batter into prepared pan, making sure not to fill the cups more than ²⁄₃ of the way as they will overflow. Bake for 25 to 35 minutes or until tops of cupcakes spring back when lightly touched. Let cool in pan on rack for 10 minutes. Carefully remove from pan and let cool completely on rack. Top cooled cupcakes with frosting.

> **Frosting suggestions:** Vegan Cream Cheese Frosting (page 184) or Vegan Chocolate Fudge Frosting (page 177).

Vegan Chocolate Raspberry Cupcakes

Makes 12 cupcakes

Here's an easy recipe for vegan chocolate cupcakes, which are awesome with raspberries. These cupcakes make a fabulous summertime dessert.

Tip

These cupcakes are delicious lightly dusted with confectioner's (icing) sugar for a super quick and simple cupcake.

- **Preheat oven to 350°F (180°C)**
- **Muffin pan, lined with paper liners**

1 1/2 cups	all-purpose flour	375 mL
1/2 cup	unsweetened Dutch-process cocoa powder, sifted	125 mL
1/2 tsp	baking soda	2 mL
Pinch	salt	Pinch
1 1/4 cups	granulated sugar	300 mL
1/2 cup	canola oil	125 mL
2/3 cup	vanilla soy milk	150 mL
1 tsp	vanilla	5 mL
3/4 cup	fresh or frozen raspberries (not thawed if frozen), optional	175 mL
1/3 cup	dairy-free semisweet chocolate chips, optional	75 mL
2 tbsp	balsamic vinegar	30 mL
	Frosting (see Frosting suggestions, below)	

1. In a bowl, whisk flour, cocoa, baking soda and salt.

2. In a large bowl, using an electric mixer or whisk, beat together sugar and oil until combined. Add soy milk and vanilla, beating just until smooth. Add flour mixture, beating just until blended. Don't overmix. Fold in raspberries, and chocolate chips, if using. Stir in balsamic vinegar.

3. Scoop batter into prepared pan, making sure not to fill the cups more than 2/3 of the way as they will overflow. Bake for 25 to 35 minutes or until tops of cupcakes spring back when lightly touched. Let cool in pan on rack for 10 minutes. Carefully remove from pan and let cool completely on rack. Top cooled cupcakes with frosting.

> **Frosting suggestions:** Vegan Cream Cheese Frosting (page 184), Vegan Fluffy Almond Cream Frosting (page 178) or Vegan Chocolate Fudge Frosting (page 177).

Vegan Cinnamon Almond Cupcakes

Makes 12 cupcakes

These subtle cupcakes have the deliciously light flavor of horchata, which is a refreshing and icy cold drink made out of ground rice and cinnamon. Horchata is a popular summer drink in Mexico, Spain and parts of South America.

Tip

If you prefer a stronger almond flavor, you can increase the amount of almond extract to 1 tsp (5 mL).

Variation

Sprinkle a few sliced almonds over the top of each unbaked cupcake or stir in $\frac{1}{3}$ to $\frac{1}{2}$ cup (75 to 125 mL) chopped almonds.

- **Preheat oven to 350°F (180°C)**
- **Muffin pan, lined with paper liners**

1 cup	soy milk	250 mL
1 tsp	apple cider vinegar	5 mL
1½ cups	all-purpose flour	375 mL
¼ cup	potato starch	60 mL
2 tsp	baking powder	10 mL
1 tsp	ground cinnamon	5 mL
¼ tsp	salt	1 mL
1 cup + 2 tbsp	granulated sugar	280 mL
½ cup	canola oil	125 mL
1 tsp	vanilla	5 mL
½ tsp	almond extract	2 mL
	Frosting (see Frosting suggestions, below)	

1. In a small bowl, whisk together soy milk and vinegar. Set aside.

2. In another bowl, whisk together flour, potato starch, baking powder, cinnamon and salt.

3. In a large bowl, whisk together half of the soy milk mixture, sugar, oil, vanilla and almond extract. Add half of the flour mixture, whisking just until incorporated. Add remaining soy milk and flour mixtures, whisking just until smooth.

4. Scoop batter into prepared pan, making sure not to fill the cups more than $\frac{2}{3}$ of the way as they will overflow. Bake for 25 to 35 minutes or until tops of cupcakes spring back when lightly touched. Let cool in pan on rack for 10 minutes. Carefully remove from pan and let cool completely on rack. Top cooled cupcakes with frosting.

> **Frosting suggestions:** Vegan Fluffy Almond Cream Frosting (page 178), Vegan Fluffy Vanilla Cream Frosting (page 183) or Vegan Cream Cheese Frosting (page 184).

Vegan Coconut Cupcakes

Makes 12 cupcakes

Eating coconut cupcakes is my way of escaping to the tropics. With each bite I can feel myself on an exotic beach, with a piña colada in my hand. The coconut milk in these cupcakes really gives them a nice subtle coconut background.

Tips

These cupcakes are best the day that they're made.

For a nice flavor finish to these cupcakes, sprinkle the frosted tops with flaked coconut.

Variation

Stir ¼ to ⅓ cup (60 to 75 mL) sweetened flaked coconut into the batter for a double coconut cupcake.

- **Preheat oven to 350°F (180°C)**
- **Muffin pan, lined with paper liners**

1 cup	canned coconut milk (not cream or cream of coconut)	250 mL
1 tsp	apple cider vinegar	5 mL
1½ cups	all-purpose flour	375 mL
¼ cup	potato starch	60 mL
2 tsp	baking powder	10 mL
Pinch	salt	Pinch
1 cup + 2 tbsp	granulated sugar	280 mL
½ cup	canola oil	125 mL
6 tbsp	soy milk	90 mL
	Frosting (see Frosting suggestions, below)	

1. In a small bowl, whisk together coconut milk and vinegar. Set aside.

2. In another bowl, whisk together flour, potato starch, baking powder and salt.

3. In a large bowl, whisk together coconut milk mixture, sugar and oil. Add half of the flour mixture, whisking just until incorporated. Add soy milk and remaining flour mixtures, whisking just until smooth.

4. Scoop batter into prepared pan, making sure not to fill the cups more than ⅔ of the way as they will overflow. Bake for 25 to 35 minutes or until tops of cupcakes spring back when lightly touched. Let cool in pan on rack for 10 minutes. Carefully remove from pan and let cool completely on rack. Top cooled cupcakes with frosting.

> **Frosting suggestions:** Vegan Fluffy Vanilla Cream Frosting (page 183), Vegan Cream Cheese Frosting (page 184) or Vegan Chocolate Fudge Frosting (page 177).

Vegan Coffee Cupcakes

This is the cupcake to bake for coffee lovers. They have a nice cinnamon coffee flavor and can be jazzed up even further with a chocolate or fluffy vanilla frosting. Plus, these cupcakes are much more fun then standing in line at your local coffeehouse.

Tip

If you want to bake these cupcakes a day ahead, they will keep well if stored in an airtight container. Brew up a large pot of coffee in the morning. Use half to drink and half for the cupcakes.

Variation

Sprinkle the tops of cupcakes with 1 tsp (5 mL) dairy-free chocolate chips.

- **Preheat oven to 350°F (180°C)**
- **2 muffin pans, lined with paper liners**

½ cup	soy milk	125 mL
1 tsp	apple cider vinegar	5 mL
1½ cups	all-purpose flour	375 mL
¼ cup	potato starch	60 mL
1 tbsp	finely ground espresso coffee	15 mL
2 tsp	baking powder	10 mL
1 tsp	ground cinnamon	5 mL
¼ tsp	salt	1 mL
1 cup + 2 tbsp	granulated sugar	280 mL
½ cup	canola oil	125 mL
½ cup	strong brewed coffee	125 mL
1 tbsp	vanilla	15 mL
	Frosting (see Frosting suggestions, below)	

1. In a small bowl, whisk together soy milk and vinegar. Set aside.

2. In another bowl, whisk together flour, potato starch, ground espresso, baking powder, cinnamon and salt.

3. In a large bowl, whisk together half of the soy milk mixture, sugar, oil, brewed coffee and vanilla. Add half of the flour mixture, whisking just until incorporated. Add remaining soy milk and flour mixtures, whisking just until smooth.

4. Scoop batter into prepared pan, making sure not to fill the cups more than ⅔ of the way as they will overflow. Bake for 25 to 35 minutes or until tops of cupcakes spring back when lightly touched. Let cool in pan on rack for 10 minutes. Carefully remove from pan and let cool completely on rack. Top cooled cupcakes with frosting.

> **Frosting suggestions:** Vegan Fluffy Vanilla Cream Frosting (page 183), Vegan Chocolate Fudge Frosting (page 177) or Vegan Cream Cheese Frosting (page 184).

Vegan Creamsicle Cupcakes

Creamsicles were my favorite ice cream pops growing up. With the delicious combination of orange sherbet and vanilla ice cream, this was the crème de la crème of frozen desserts. Here I've combined those fab flavors into my new favorite cupcake.

- **Preheat oven to 350°F (180°C)**
- **Muffin pan, lined with paper liners**

¾ cup	soy milk	175 mL
1 tsp	apple cider vinegar	5 mL
1½ cups	all-purpose flour	375 mL
¼ cup	potato starch	60 mL
2 tsp	baking powder	10 mL
¼ tsp	salt	1 mL
1 cup + 2 tbsp	granulated sugar	280 mL
½ cup	canola oil	125 mL
2 tbsp	frozen orange juice concentrate, thawed	30 mL
1 tbsp	vanilla	15 mL
¼ tsp	pure orange oil	1 mL
	Frosting (see Frosting suggestions, below)	

1. In a small bowl, whisk together soy milk and vinegar. Set aside.

2. In another bowl, whisk together flour, potato starch, baking powder and salt.

3. In a large bowl, whisk together sugar, oil, orange juice concentrate, vanilla, orange oil and half of the soy milk mixture. Whisk until smooth. Add half of the flour mixture, whisking just until incorporated. Add remaining soy milk and flour mixtures, whisking just until smooth.

4. Scoop batter into prepared pan, making sure not to fill the cups more than ⅔ of the way as they will overflow. Bake for 25 to 35 minutes or until tops of cupcakes spring back when lightly touched. Let cool in pan on rack for 10 minutes. Carefully remove from pan and let cool completely on rack. Top cooled cupcakes with frosting.

> **Frosting suggestions:** Vegan Fluffy Vanilla Cream Frosting (page 183) or Vegan Chocolate Fudge Frosting (page 177).

Vegan Green Tea Matcha Cupcakes

Makes 12 cupcakes

If you're a fan of matcha tea lattes, you will love the flavor of these cupcakes. They have a gorgeous green color and a nice light matcha flavor.

Tip

If you want a slightly deeper matcha flavor, you can add in another teaspoon (5 mL) or more to taste. Be careful not too add too much though as the matcha can make the cupcakes very bitter.

- Preheat oven to 350°F (180°C)
- Muffin pan, lined with paper liners

1 cup	soy milk	250 mL
1 tsp	apple cider vinegar	5 mL
1½ cups	all-purpose flour	375 mL
¼ cup	potato starch	60 mL
2 tsp	baking powder	10 mL
¼ tsp	salt	1 mL
1 cup + 2 tbsp	granulated sugar	280 mL
½ cup	canola oil	125 mL
1 tbsp	matcha green tea powder	15 mL
	Frosting (see Frosting suggestions, below)	

1. In a small bowl, whisk together soy milk and vinegar. Set aside.

2. In another bowl, whisk together flour, potato starch, baking powder and salt.

3. In a large bowl, whisk together sugar, oil, matcha powder and half of the soy milk mixture. Whisk until smooth and matcha powder is dissolved. Add half of the flour mixture, whisking just until incorporated. Add remaining soy milk and flour mixtures, whisking just until smooth.

4. Scoop batter into prepared pan, making sure not to fill the cups more than ⅔ of the way as they will overflow. Bake for 25 to 35 minutes or until tops of cupcakes spring back when lightly touched. Let cool in pan on rack for 10 minutes. Carefully remove from pan and let cool completely on rack. Top cooled cupcakes with frosting.

> **Frosting suggestions:** Vegan Fluffy Vanilla Cream Frosting (page 183) or Vegan Cream Cheese Frosting (page 184).

Vegan Lemon Cupcakes

These cupcakes have been a huge hit at our food cart, Native Bowl, in Portland, Oregon. The cupcakes have a nice delicate crumb, with the vibrant flavor of lemon. I bet you can't have just one!

Tip

Make sure to divide the batter evenly among the muffin cups.

Variation

For an orange version, substitute about ½ tsp (2 mL) of pure orange oil for the lemon.

- **Preheat oven to 350°F (180°C)**
- **Muffin pan, lined with paper liners**

1 cup	soy milk	250 mL
1 tsp	apple cider vinegar	5 mL
1½ cups	all-purpose flour	375 mL
¼ cup	potato starch	60 mL
2 tsp	baking powder	10 mL
¼ tsp	salt	1 mL
1 cup + 2 tbsp	granulated sugar	280 mL
½ cup	canola oil	125 mL
	Finely grated zest of 1 lemon	
¾ tsp	pure lemon oil	3 mL
	Frosting (see Frosting suggestions, below)	

1. In a small bowl, whisk together soy milk and vinegar. Set aside.

2. In another bowl, whisk together flour, potato starch, baking powder and salt.

3. In a large bowl, whisk together half of the soy milk mixture, sugar, oil, lemon zest and lemon oil. Add half of the flour mixture, whisking just until incorporated. Add remaining soy milk and flour mixtures, whisking just until smooth.

4. Scoop batter into prepared pan, making sure not to fill the cups more than ⅔ of the way as they will overflow. Bake for 25 to 35 minutes or until tops of cupcakes spring back when lightly touched. Let cool in pan on rack for 10 minutes. Carefully remove from pan and let cool completely on rack. Top cooled cupcakes with frosting.

> **Frosting suggestions:** Vegan Fluffy Lemon Cream Frosting (page 179), Vegan Fluffy Vanilla Cream Frosting (page 183), Vegan Chocolate Fudge Frosting (page 177) or Vegan Cream Cheese Frosting (page 184).

Vegan Mocha Cupcakes

To me, these cupcakes make a perfect breakfast. You get your coffee and pastry all in one. They are the perfect combination of chocolate, coffee, cinnamon, vanilla and a hint of orange.

Tip

The chocolate chips might make the tops of cupcakes sink in a little, which can be easily covered with a little frosting.

Variation

You can leave out the orange oil and chocolate chips, if desired.

- **Preheat oven to 350°F (180°C)**
- **Muffin pan, lined with paper liners**

1 cup	soy milk	250 mL
1 tsp	apple cider vinegar	5 mL
1 cup	all-purpose flour	250 mL
½ cup	unsweetened Dutch-process cocoa powder, sifted	125 mL
¼ cup	potato starch	60 mL
2 tbsp	finely ground espresso	30 mL
1 tbsp	instant coffee granules	15 mL
2 tsp	baking powder	10 mL
1 tsp	ground cinnamon	5 mL
¼ tsp	salt	1 mL
1 cup + 2 tbsp	granulated sugar	280 mL
½ cup	canola oil	125 mL
1 tbsp	vanilla	15 mL
¼ tsp	pure orange oil	1 mL
½ cup	dairy-free semisweet chocolate chips, optional	125 mL
	Frosting (see suggestions, below)	

1. In a small bowl, whisk together soy milk and vinegar.

2. In another bowl, whisk together flour, cocoa, potato starch, espresso, instant coffee, baking powder, cinnamon and salt.

3. In a large bowl, whisk together half of the soy milk mixture, sugar, oil, vanilla and orange oil. Add half of the flour mixture, whisking just until incorporated. Add remaining soy milk and flour mixtures, whisking just until smooth. Fold in chocolate chips, if using.

4. Scoop batter into prepared pan, making sure not to fill the cups more than ⅔ of the way as they will overflow. Bake for 25 to 35 minutes or until tops of cupcakes spring back when lightly touched. Let cool in pan on rack for 10 minutes. Carefully remove from pan and let cool completely on rack. Top cooled cupcakes with frosting.

> **Frosting suggestions:** Vegan Fluffy Vanilla Cream Frosting (page 183) or Vegan Chocolate Fudge Frosting (page 177).

Vegan Oat Spice Cupcakes

These are a lightly and deliciously spiced cupcake that taste just like an oatmeal cookie. If you use certified gluten-free oat flour, they are gluten-free as well. The cupcakes are a touch crumbly, but topped with a dollop of buttercream, they will disappear faster than Houdini.

Tip

If you can't find oat flour, you can grind your own in a powerful blender. Just make sure to grind it until it's a superfine flour.

Variation

Stir ⅓ to ½ cup (75 to 125 mL) raisins into the batter for an oatmeal cookie version.

- **Preheat oven to 350°F (180°C)**
- **Muffin pan, lined with paper liners**

1 cup	soy milk	250 mL
1 tsp	apple cider vinegar	5 mL
2 cups	oat flour	500 mL
¼ cup	potato starch	60 mL
2 tsp	baking powder	10 mL
1 tsp	ground cinnamon	5 mL
½ tsp	ground allspice	2 mL
½ tsp	ground nutmeg	2 mL
½ tsp	xanthan gum	2 mL
¼ tsp	salt	1 mL
½ cup	granulated sugar	125 mL
½ cup	packed brown sugar	125 mL
½ cup	canola oil	125 mL
	Frosting (see suggestions, below)	

1. In a small bowl, whisk together soy milk and vinegar. Set aside.

2. In another bowl, whisk together oat flour, potato starch, baking powder, cinnamon, allspice, nutmeg, xanthan gum and salt.

3. In a large bowl, whisk together granulated and brown sugars, oil and half of the soy milk mixture. Whisk until smooth. Add half of the flour mixture, whisking just until incorporated. Add remaining soy milk and flour mixtures, whisking just until smooth.

4. Scoop batter into prepared pan, making sure not to fill the cups more than ⅔ of the way as they will overflow. Bake for 25 to 35 minutes or until tops of cupcakes spring back when lightly touched. Let cool in pan on rack for 10 minutes. Carefully remove from pan and let cool completely on rack. Top cooled cupcakes with frosting.

> **Frosting suggestions:** Vegan Cream Cheese Frosting (page 184), Vegan Fluffy Vanilla Cream Frosting (page 183) or Vegan Chocolate Fudge Frosting (page 177).

Vegan Pumpkin Pecan Cupcakes

Makes 12 cupcakes

Hands down, this is my son's favorite cupcake. I tend to bake pumpkin desserts primarily in the fall, but really I should be making them year-round. This is a nice and tender cupcake with a good balance of spices and pumpkin flavor.

Tip

These cupcakes can be made a day ahead. Just make sure to store in a sealed container.

Variation

Add ½ cup (125 mL) raisins into the batter instead of the pecans.

- **Preheat oven to 350°F (180°C)**
- **Muffin pan, lined with paper liners**

1 cup	soy milk	250 mL
1 tsp	apple cider vinegar	5 mL
1½ cups	all-purpose flour	375 mL
¼ cup	potato starch	60 mL
2 tsp	baking powder	10 mL
1½ tsp	ground cinnamon	7 mL
1 tsp	ground allspice	5 mL
½ tsp	ground nutmeg	2 mL
¼ tsp	salt	1 mL
1½ cups	granulated sugar	375 mL
¾ cup	canned pumpkin purée (not pumpkin pie filling)	175 mL
½ cup	canola oil	125 mL
½ cup	chopped lightly toasted pecans, optional	125 mL
	Frosting (see suggestions, below)	

1. In a small bowl, whisk together soy milk and vinegar.

2. In another bowl, whisk flour, potato starch, baking powder, cinnamon, allspice, nutmeg and salt.

3. In a large bowl, whisk together sugar, pumpkin and oil. Whisk in half of the soy milk mixture. Whisk until smooth. Add half of the flour mixture, whisking just until incorporated. Add remaining soy milk, flour and pecans, whisking just until smooth.

4. Scoop batter into prepared pan, making sure not to fill the cups more than ⅔ of the way as they will overflow. Bake for 30 to 35 minutes or until tops of cupcakes spring back when lightly touched. Let cool in pan on rack for 10 minutes. Carefully remove from pan and let cool completely on rack. Top cooled cupcakes with frosting.

> **Frosting suggestions:** Vegan Cream Cheese Frosting (page 184) or Vegan Fluffy Vanilla Cream Frosting (page 183).

Vegan Sweet Vanilla Cupcakes

Makes 12 cupcakes

Along with a great chocolate cupcake recipe, a fabulous vanilla cupcake recipe is essential, too. These cupcakes have a nice vanilla flavor and a delicate and soft crumb.

Tip

Make sure to divide the batter evenly among the muffin cups. These cupcakes are really good filled with apricot, blackberry or raspberry jam.

Variation

Carefully fold ¾ cup (175 mL) fresh raspberries into the batter for a raspberry vanilla cupcake.

- **Preheat oven to 350°F (180°C)**
- **Muffin pan, lined with paper liners**

1 cup	soy milk	250 mL
1 tsp	apple cider vinegar	5 mL
1½ cups	all-purpose flour	375 mL
¼ cup	potato starch	60 mL
2 tsp	baking powder	10 mL
¼ tsp	salt	1 mL
1 cup + 2 tbsp	granulated sugar	300 mL
½ cup	canola oil	125 mL
2 tbsp	vanilla	30 mL
	Frosting (see suggestions, below)	

1. In a small bowl, whisk together soy milk and vinegar. Set aside.

2. In another bowl, whisk together flour, potato starch, baking powder and salt.

3. In a large bowl, whisk together sugar, oil, vanilla and half of the reserved soy milk. Whisk until smooth. Add half of the flour mixture, whisking just until incorporated. Add remaining soy milk and flour, whisking just until smooth.

4. Scoop batter into prepared pan, making sure not to fill the cups more than ⅔ of the way as they will overflow. Bake for 25 to 35 minutes or until tops of cupcakes spring back when lightly touched. Let cool in pan on rack for 10 minutes. Carefully remove from pan and let cool completely on rack. Top cooled cupcakes with frosting.

> **Frosting suggestions:** Vegan Fluffy Almond Cream Frosting (page 178), Vegan Fluffy Vanilla Cream Frosting (page 183), Vegan Chocolate Fudge Frosting (page 177), Vegan Peanut Butter Frosting (page 182), Vegan Cream Cheese Frosting (page 184) or Vegan Fluffy Lemon Cream Frosting (page 179).

Vegan Toasted Sesame Cupcakes

Makes 12 cupcakes

These cupcakes have a really nice toasted sesame flavor, with a light and delicate crumb. When I served these at our food cart, Native Bowl, customers went crazy for their exotic flavor.

Tip

Make sure to divide the batter evenly among the cupcakes. Garnish the frosted cupcakes with a tiny sprinkle of toasted sesame seeds.

Variation

You can substitute half black sesame seeds for half of the white for a fun speckled effect.

- **Preheat oven to 350°F (180°C)**
- **Muffin pan, lined with paper liners**

1 cup	soy milk	250 mL
1 tsp	apple cider vinegar	5 mL
1½ cups	all-purpose flour	375 mL
⅓ cup	toasted white sesame seeds	75 mL
¼ cup	potato starch	60 mL
2 tsp	baking powder	10 mL
Pinch	salt	Pinch
1 cup + 2 tbsp	granulated sugar	280 mL
⅓ cup	canola oil	75 mL
3 tbsp	toasted sesame oil	45 mL
	Frosting (see Frosting suggestions, below)	

1. In a small bowl, whisk together soy milk and vinegar. Set aside.

2. In another bowl, whisk together flour, sesame seeds, potato starch, baking powder and salt.

3. In a large bowl, whisk together half of the soy milk mixture, sugar, canola oil and sesame oil. Add half of the flour mixture, whisking just until incorporated. Add remaining soy milk and flour mixtures, whisking just until smooth.

4. Scoop batter into prepared pan, making sure not to fill the cups more than ⅔ of the way as they will overflow. Bake for 25 to 35 minutes or until tops of cupcakes spring back when lightly touched. Let cool in pan on rack for 10 minutes. Carefully remove from pan and let cool completely on rack. Top cooled cupcakes with frosting.

> **Frosting suggestions:** Vegan Fluffy Almond Cream Frosting (page 178), Vegan Fluffy Vanilla Cream Frosting (page 183) or Vegan Cream Cheese Frosting (page 184).

Frostings, Glazes and Fillings

Caramel Frosting............ 148

Chocolate Fudge Frosting 149

Chocolate Glaze 150

Chocolate Mousse Filling 151

Chocolate Hazelnut Frosting... 152

Chocolate Toffee Sauce 153

Coconut Pecan Frosting....... 154

Coffee Buttercream 155

Coffee Ice Cream 156

Cookies and Cream
   Buttercream 157

Cream Cheese Icing.......... 158

Easy Buttercream Frosting.... 159

Vanilla Cream Frosting....... 160

Ginger Cream Cheese Icing ... 161

Honey Cream Cheese Frosting.. 162

Hot Fudge Sauce 163

Lemon Cream............... 164

Lemon Curd 165

Malted Milk Espresso Icing ... 166

Maple Buttercream 167

Orange Cream Cheese Icing ... 168

Peanut Butter Frosting 169

Peanut Butter Fudge Frosting . 170

Rum Buttercream 171

Strawberry Cream Cheese
   Buttercream 172

Vanilla Ice Cream 173

Vanilla Custard Filling....... 174

Whipped Cream Topping...... 175

Vegan Chocolate Icing 176

Vegan Chocolate Fudge
   Frosting.................. 177

Vegan Fluffy Almond Cream
   Frosting.................. 178

Vegan Fluffy Lemon Cream
   Frosting.................. 179

Vegan Large Batch Fluffy
   Frosting.................. 180

Vegan Lemon Glaze.......... 181

Vegan Peanut Butter Frosting . 182

Vegan Fluffy Vanilla Cream
   Frosting.................. 183

Vegan Cream Cheese Frosting . 184

Caramel Frosting

This frosting is adapted from a recipe by Donna Hay. Her delicious concoctions are a constant source of inspiration, and this one is a true winner. I've added corn syrup to the caramel because it renders the texture silky smooth.

Tips

Usually 1 cup (250 mL) of frosting is only enough to frost about 8 cupcakes. This frosting is so rich, though, that you can frost 12 cupcakes with it.

Make the frosting before baking the cupcakes so the caramel has time to cool.

1 cup	whipping (35%) cream	250 mL
½ cup	packed light brown sugar	125 mL
¼ cup	light corn syrup	60 mL
1 tbsp	unsalted butter	15 mL
¼ tsp	salt	1 mL

1. In a heavy saucepan, combine cream, brown sugar, corn syrup, butter and salt. Heat over medium-high heat, stirring, for 2 minutes or until sugar is dissolved and butter is melted.

2. Reduce heat to medium. Cook, stirring often, for 10 to 15 minutes or until thickened. Remove from heat. Stir until smooth and pour into a bowl. Let cool in bowl, stirring occasionally. Caramel will thicken further as it sits and cools.

3. Stir cooled caramel well and spread or spoon over cooled cupcakes.

Chocolate Fudge Frosting

*As far as chocolate
frostings go, this is one of
my all-time, hands-down
favorites. My mom made
this frosting all the time
when I was growing up. It
goes together quickly and is
outrageously chocolaty.*

Tip

Extra frosting will keep in
an airtight container in the
refrigerator for several days.
Let soften and stir until
smooth before spreading.

Variation

If you prefer your frosting
a little less sweet, you can
reduce the confectioner's
sugar by ½ cup (125 mL)
for the full recipe or ¼ cup
(60 mL) for half the recipe.

1½ cups	confectioner's (icing) sugar	375 mL
¾ cup	unsweetened Dutch-process cocoa powder, sifted	175 mL
½ cup	unsalted butter, at room temperature	125 mL
2 tbsp	chocolate cream liqueur	30 mL
1 tbsp	strong brewed coffee or milk	15 mL
Pinch	salt	Pinch

1. In a food processor fitted with a metal blade, process confectioner's sugar, cocoa powder, butter, chocolate liqueur, coffee and salt until smooth, scraping down sides as necessary.

2. Spread frosting on cooled cupcakes.

Chocolate Glaze

This is a very quick and chocolaty topping for cupcakes when you don't have time to make a buttercream. This glaze, also known as a ganache, gives an elegant look to your homemade cupcakes.

Variation

Substitute chopped semisweet chocolate for the chocolate chips.

| ½ cup | semisweet chocolate chips | 125 mL |
| ⅓ cup | whipping (35%) cream | 75 mL |

1. In a microwave-safe bowl, combine chocolate chips and cream. Microwave, uncovered, on High for 30 to 60 seconds or until cream is hot and chocolate starts to melt. Stir until chocolate is melted and mixture is thick and smooth.

2. If chocolate is not completely melted, return to microwave for another 10 to 20 seconds or until chocolate is soft and melted. Stir well. Let glaze sit for a few minutes to thicken slightly. Pour glaze over tops of cooled cupcakes.

3. Refrigerate cupcakes until glaze is firm.

Chocolate Mousse Filling

Here's a gem of a filling from my first cookbook, 125 Best Chocolate Chip Recipes. Not only is it fairly quick to create, but it also makes a delicious addition to just about any cupcake. And I do mean any cupcake. Trust me on this one!

Tip

Plan on making this filling within several hours of using to fill cupcakes.

⅓ cup	semisweet chocolate chips	75 mL
1 tbsp	strong brewed coffee	15 mL
¾ cup	whipping (35%) cream	175 mL
1 tbsp	confectioner's (icing) sugar	15 mL

1. In a microwave-safe bowl, combine chocolate chips and coffee. Microwave, uncovered, on High for 20 to 30 seconds or until chocolate is shiny and almost melted. Stir until smooth. Let cool slightly.

2. In a large bowl, using an electric mixer, whip cream and confectioner's sugar just until stiff peaks form. Add melted chocolate mixture to cream mixture, beating just until incorporated.

3. *To fill cupcakes:* Slice cupcakes in half horizontally, spreading filling on bottom halves of cupcakes and replacing tops over filling. Or, using a sharp paring knife, gently cut a ¾-inch (2 cm) diameter cone from the bottom of each cupcake and trim point off cone. Using a small spoon, fill each hole with Chocolate Mousse Filling and replace reserved cones.

Chocolate Hazelnut Frosting

**Makes about
2 cups (500 mL),
enough to frost
16 or more cupcakes**

Can chocolate and hazelnut ever be bad? Well, the answer is an emphatic and resounding "NO!" But you can make them even better when you whip them into a fudgy frosting.

Tip

Extra frosting will keep in an airtight container in the refrigerator for 2 days. Let soften before spreading.

½ cup	unsalted butter, at room temperature	125 mL
1 cup	confectioner's (icing) sugar	250 mL
¾ cup	unsweetened Dutch-process cocoa powder, sifted	175 mL
Pinch	salt	Pinch
¾ cup	chocolate hazelnut spread, such as Nutella	175 mL
3 tbsp	whipping (35%) cream	45 mL

1. In a bowl, using an electric mixer on high speed, beat butter until fluffy, scraping down sides of bowl as necessary.

2. With mixer on low speed, beat in confectioner's sugar in two additions so the sugar doesn't fly all over the place. Add cocoa powder and salt and beat until smooth. Add chocolate hazelnut spread and whipping cream, beating well. Increase speed to medium-high and beat until light and fluffy.

3. Spread frosting over cooled cupcakes and refrigerate until ready to serve for up to 1 day.

Chocolate Toffee Sauce

Makes about 1½ cups (375 mL), enough to drizzle over 12 to 24 cupcakes

This recipe was adapted from a tried-and-true toffee sauce recipe by Jill Dupleix. I've added a hint of chocolate, but you can certainly omit it for a non-chocolate version.

1 cup	whipping (35%) cream	250 mL
¾ cup	packed light brown sugar	175 mL
2 tbsp	light corn syrup	30 mL
2 tbsp	unsalted butter	30 mL
Pinch	salt	Pinch
1 oz	unsweetened chocolate, chopped	30 g
1 tsp	vanilla	5 mL

1. In a heavy saucepan, whisk together cream, brown sugar, corn syrup, butter and salt. Butter will be lumpy, but don't worry.

2. Place saucepan over medium heat and bring to a simmer, whisking constantly. If mixture starts to boil rapidly, reduce heat to maintain a simmer. Simmer for 5 minutes. Remove from heat.

3. Whisk in chocolate and vanilla until smooth. Spoon hot toffee sauce over warm cupcakes and serve immediately.

Coconut Pecan Frosting

If you love German chocolate cake or are a big fan of caramel and coconut, I promise you that you're going to love this frosting. It is truly divine! I find it hard to not eat this frosting with a ladle.

Tips

This frosting will keep in an airtight container in the refrigerator for up to 2 days.

If the mixture is too thick, thin with an additional spoonful or two of canned milk to achieve a spreadable consistency.

½ cup	packed light brown sugar	125 mL
1 tbsp	cornstarch	15 mL
Pinch	salt	Pinch
1 cup	evaporated milk	250 mL
¼ cup	unsalted butter, at room temperature	60 mL
½ cup	loosely packed sweetened flaked coconut	125 mL
½ tsp	vanilla	2 mL
½ cup	toasted chopped pecans (see Nuts, page 14)	125 mL
⅓ cup	semisweet chocolate chips, optional	75 mL

1. In a heavy saucepan, whisk together brown sugar, cornstarch and salt. Slowly whisk in evaporated milk until cornstarch is dissolved. Add butter. Butter will be lumpy, but don't worry, it will melt from the heat.

2. Place saucepan over medium heat. Cook, whisking until butter is melted and mixture is smooth. Whisk continuously until mixture is very thick. Remove from heat. Stir in coconut and vanilla. Transfer to a bowl and let cool to room temperature.

3. Cover coconut mixture with plastic wrap and refrigerate for 2 hours or until chilled and thick. When cold and thick, stir in pecans and chocolate chips, if using. Spread frosting over cooled cupcakes. If not serving cupcakes right away, keep cupcakes refrigerated until ready to serve or for up to 1 day.

Coffee Buttercream

*When you combine
the bold, rich flavor
of coffee with the delicate
sweetness of buttercream,
you have the frosting
of champions. This luscious
frosting is destined to
become a staple for coffee
lovers everywhere. Just ask
my brother, Jon, who has
become addicted to it.*

1 cup	unsalted butter, at room temperature	250 mL
3 cups	confectioner's (icing) sugar	750 mL
Pinch	salt	Pinch
1 tsp	vanilla	5 mL
1 tbsp	instant coffee granules	15 mL
1 tsp	hot coffee	5 mL
1 tsp	coffee-flavored liqueur, such as Kahlúa	5 mL

1. In a small bowl, using an electric mixer on low speed, beat together butter, sugar and salt until well combined. Increase speed to high and beat until light and fluffy. Add vanilla, beating until frosting is smooth.

2. In a small bowl, whisk together coffee granules, hot coffee and liqueur. Stir until coffee granules are dissolved. Let cool completely.

3. Add cooled coffee mixture to butter mixture, beating until smooth, creamy and well mixed. You will need to scrape down sides of bowl several times while mixing.

4. Spread icing over cooled cupcakes with a knife or place in a pastry bag and pipe decoratively over cupcakes.

Coffee Ice Cream

This is a fun way to top your cupcakes! It's simple: just scoop or swirl homemade ice cream onto the tops of your cupcakes. You will never think of frosting the same way again.

Tips

Spread slightly softened ice cream over tops of cupcakes instead of frosting, or top baked cupcakes with a scoop of ice cream. Just make sure to serve immediately or place in freezer until ready to serve.

Store ice cream in the freezer for up to 1 day in an airtight container with a piece of plastic wrap pressed onto the surface. Homemade ice cream is best the day that it's made.

Variation

For a chocolate chip version, add $1/2$ cup (125 mL) miniature semisweet chocolate chips during the last 5 minutes of freezing.

- **Ice cream maker**

$1^1/_2$ cups	milk, divided	375 mL
$1/_4$ cup	ground dark roast coffee	60 mL
1 tbsp	instant coffee granules	15 mL
$1^3/_4$ cups	whipping (35%) cream	425 mL
$1/_2$ cup	superfine sugar (see Tips, page 64)	125 mL
1 tsp	vanilla paste or extract (see Tip, page 28)	5 mL

1. In a small heavy saucepan, combine $1/2$ cup (125 mL) of the milk and ground and instant coffees. Bring mixture to a simmer over medium heat. Let cool to room temperature.

2. In a bowl, whisk together cream, remaining 1 cup (250 mL) milk, sugar and vanilla paste until combined and sugar is dissolved. Strain cooled coffee mixture into cream mixture, whisking well.

3. Pour mixture into an ice cream maker and freeze according to manufacturer's directions. Serve immediately or freeze in an airtight container (see Tips, left).

Cookies and Cream Buttercream

Cookies and cream is always a crowd-pleaser, making this a winning icing. It's not too sweet, which is a nice change from most icings.

Variation

You can increase the sugar in this recipe to 1½ cups (375 mL) for a sweeter icing.

1⅓ cups	confectioner's (icing) sugar	325 mL
½ cup	unsalted butter, at room temperature	125 mL
Pinch	salt	Pinch
⅓ cup	whipping (35%) cream	75 mL
½ tsp	vanilla	2 mL
4	chocolate sandwich cookies, broken into pieces	4

1. In a small bowl, using an electric mixer on low speed, beat together sugar, butter and salt until well combined. Increase speed to high, beating until light and fluffy. Add cream and vanilla, beating until frosting is smooth. Add broken cookies, beating until mixed.

2. Spread icing on cooled cupcakes with a knife.

Cream Cheese Icing

*Cream cheese icing
tastes great on just about
everything. It's a quick mix
that can make something
go from tasting good to
tasting extraordinary.*

Tips

Because cream cheese
is perishable, be sure
to keep your frosted
cupcakes refrigerated until
you're ready to eat them.

This frosting will keep in
an airtight container in
the refrigerator for up to
3 days. Before using, let
stand at room temperature
for 15 minutes to soften
enough to spread.

Variation

Add a drop of food coloring
to the frosting as you
are making it for a touch
of beautiful color.

4 oz	cream cheese, at room temperature	125 g
1/2 cup	unsalted butter, at room temperature	125 mL
Pinch	salt	Pinch
2 1/4 cups	confectioner's (icing) sugar, sifted	550 mL

1. In a bowl, using an electric mixer on medium-high speed, beat together cream cheese, butter and salt until creamy. With mixer on low speed, beat in confectioner's sugar, 1/2 cup (125 mL) at a time so that the sugar doesn't fly all over the place. Increase speed to medium-high and beat until light and fluffy.

2. Spread frosting over cooled cupcakes and refrigerate until ready to serve or for up to 1 day.

Easy Buttercream Frosting

This sweet, creamy white icing works well on almost any cupcake. When kids scream for white frosting, this is your ticket. When the mood strikes, you can add a drop of food coloring to tint it almost any color of the rainbow.

Tip

This frosting is best made just before you're ready to use it.

Variations

For a minty flavor and green color, add a drop of peppermint extract and green food coloring.

Omit the vanilla extract. Use vanilla paste (see Tip, page 28) instead of the vanilla extract.

3 cups	confectioner's (icing) sugar	750 mL
1 cup	unsalted butter, at room temperature	250 mL
Pinch	salt	Pinch
1 tsp	vanilla	5 mL

1. In a small bowl, using an electric mixer on low speed, beat together sugar, butter and salt until creamy. Increase speed to high and beat until light and fluffy. Add vanilla, beating until frosting is smooth.

2. Spread icing on cooled cupcakes with a knife or transfer to a pastry bag and pipe decoratively over cupcakes.

Vanilla Cream Frosting

This is a seriously delicious and super-easy frosting for cupcakes. It assembles very quickly and has a light and creamy vanilla taste. This is not your ordinary cloyingly sweet icing: it will please the discerning palates of kids and adults alike.

Tip

This frosting is best made just before you're ready to use it.

Variation

Tint the frosting with food coloring. Be careful not to use too much color. Start with a drop, mix it in well, and add more only if necessary.

1⅓ cups	confectioner's (icing) sugar	325 mL
½ cup	unsalted butter, at room temperature	125 mL
Pinch	salt	Pinch
⅓ cup	whipping (35%) cream	75 mL
½ tsp	vanilla paste or vanilla (see Tip, page 28)	2 mL

1. In a small bowl, using an electric mixer on low speed, beat together sugar, butter and salt until creamy. Increase speed to high and beat until light and fluffy. Add cream and vanilla paste, beating until frosting is smooth.

2. Spread icing on cooled cupcakes with a knife or transfer to a pastry bag and pipe decoratively over cupcakes.

Pink Lemonade Cupcakes (page 88)

Carrot Cupcakes (page 93)

Pumpkin Cupcakes (page 98)

Raspberry Vanilla Cupcakes (page 107)

Lamington Cupcakes (page 108)

Lemon Cheesecake Cupcakes (page 113)

Carrot Zucchini Cupcakes (page 117)

White Cupcakes with Coconut Frosting (page 116)

Sticky Date Cupcakes (page 119)

Ginger Cream Cheese Icing

This delicious icing gives that extra-special bite that punches up the flavors of carrot cupcakes, ginger cupcakes and even chocolate cupcakes.

Tip

This frosting will keep in an airtight container in the refrigerator for up to 2 days. Before using, let stand at room temperature for 15 minutes to soften enough to spread.

4 oz	cream cheese, at room temperature	125 g
$\frac{1}{4}$ cup	unsalted butter, at room temperature	60 mL
2$\frac{1}{4}$ cups	confectioner's (icing) sugar, sifted	550 mL
$\frac{1}{4}$ cup	finely chopped crystallized ginger	60 mL
1 tsp	ground ginger	5 mL
Pinch	salt	Pinch

1. In a bowl, using an electric mixer on medium-high speed, beat together cream cheese and butter until creamy. With mixer on low speed, beat in confectioner's sugar, $\frac{1}{2}$ cup (125 mL) at a time so that the sugar doesn't fly all over the place. Increase speed to medium-high, beating until light and fluffy. Add crystallized ginger, ground ginger and salt, beating until well mixed.

2. Spread frosting over cupcakes and refrigerate until ready to serve or for up to 8 hours.

Honey Cream Cheese Frosting

This sweet frosting is a close runner-up to honey butter. It is very soft, delicate and pleasing to sink your teeth into. To achieve the right texture, make sure to refrigerate it until it is thick enough to spread.

Tip

Transfer frosting to an airtight container and refrigerate until you're ready to use it.

8 oz	cream cheese, at room temperature	250 g
½ cup	unsalted butter, at room temperature	125 mL
Pinch	salt	Pinch
1 cup	confectioner's (icing) sugar	250 mL
⅓ cup	liquid honey	75 mL

1. In a bowl, using an electric mixer on high speed, beat together cream cheese, butter and salt until fluffy.

2. With mixer on low speed, beat in confectioner's sugar, ⅓ cup (75 mL) at a time so that the sugar doesn't fly all over the place. Add honey, beating well. Increase speed to medium-high and beat until light and fluffy.

3. Cover and refrigerate frosting for 2 to 3 hours or until firm enough to spread, or overnight. Spread frosting over cupcakes and refrigerate until ready to serve or for up to 8 hours.

Hot Fudge Sauce

*My friend Tamara gave me
this recipe years ago. I'm
not sure where she found
it, but I do know that it's
delicious beyond words and
obscenely fantastic drizzled
over cupcakes.*

Tip

Store cooled fudge sauce in
a canning jar covered with
a lid in the refrigerator for
up to 1 week. To reheat,
remove lid and microwave
until warm.

Variation

Add ½ cup (125 mL) raisins
or dried cherries along with
cream in Step 1.

½ cup	packed light brown sugar	125 mL
½ cup	whipping (35%) cream	125 mL
¼ cup	unsalted butter	60 mL
Pinch	salt	Pinch
½ cup	unsweetened Dutch-process cocoa powder, sifted	125 mL
1 tbsp	dark rum	15 mL

1. In a heavy saucepan, whisk together brown sugar, cream, butter and salt until combined. Bring cream mixture to a simmer over medium-high heat, whisking occasionally. Reduce heat to medium-low and whisk in cocoa powder.

2. Remove saucepan from heat and whisk in rum. Let fudge sauce cool just until thickened. Spoon over cupcakes. Fudge sauce will become very thick as it cools further.

Lemon Cream

*Hello, calling all lemon
lovers! This ethereal,
cloudlike topping is
heavenly on cupcakes.
It's also delicious topped
with a sprinkling of fresh
raspberries or blueberries.*

Tip

If you prefer a slightly
sweeter topping, you can
increase the confectioner's
sugar to ¼ cup (60 mL).

Variation

Add a tiny drop of yellow
food coloring for a brighter
color.

⅔ cup	whipping (35%) cream	150 mL
3 tbsp	confectioner's (icing) sugar	45 mL
1 tsp	grated lemon zest	5 mL
½ cup	lemon curd, homemade (see recipe, page 165) or store-bought	125 mL

1. In a bowl, using an electric mixer, whip together cream, confectioner's sugar and lemon zest just until stiff peaks form.

2. Gently fold lemon curd into whipped cream mixture. Spread or dollop over cooled cupcakes right before serving. If making ahead, refrigerate lemon cream in an airtight container for up to 2 hours and spread on cupcakes just before serving. It is best used the day it's made.

Lemon Curd

Makes about 1⅓ cups (325 mL), enough to fill 16 or more cupcakes

This flavorful, tangy lemon curd is adapted from a recipe in Gourmet *magazine. It's a snap to prepare. I dub this topping "nectar of the gods," and it's best applied to lemon or vanilla cupcakes.*

Tips

Make sure that the egg yolks are at room temperature to help prevent the lemon curd from curdling. The lemon curd can be covered and refrigerated for up to 1 week. If your lemon curd does curdle slightly, strain the warm curd into a bowl and let cool. Proceed with recipe.

Use the chilled lemon curd as a cupcake filling.

Variation

Substitute lime zest and lime juice for the lemon zest and lemon juice.

½ cup	superfine sugar (see Tips, page 64)	125 mL
1 tsp	cornstarch	5 mL
2 tsp	finely grated lemon zest	10 mL
½ cup	freshly squeezed lemon juice	125 mL
4	egg yolks	4
6 tbsp	unsalted butter, chilled and cut into pieces	90 mL

1. In a heavy saucepan, whisk together sugar and cornstarch. Whisk in lemon zest and juice and egg yolks until well combined. Whisk in butter and cook over medium-low heat, whisking constantly, for 6 minutes or until lemon mixture is thick enough to hold marks of whisk.

2. Transfer lemon curd to a bowl, placing plastic wrap directly on surface. Refrigerate for 1 hour or until cold.

Malted Milk Espresso Icing

Makes about ⅔ cup (150 mL), enough to frost 12 cupcakes

Wow! There's a new kid on the block here. This icing is quick and easy and adds an extra dimension to plain cupcakes.

Tip

This icing cannot be made ahead of time because it will harden and crack. Make right before you're ready to use it.

2 tbsp + 1 tsp	strong brewed coffee (approx.)	35 mL
2 tbsp	malted milk powder (see Tip, page 68)	30 mL
1½ cups	confectioner's (icing) sugar	375 mL

1. In a small cup, whisk together 2 tbsp (30 mL) coffee and malted milk powder until powder is dissolved.

2. In a bowl, whisk together confectioner's sugar and coffee mixture until smooth, adding more coffee if necessary to achieve desired consistency.

3. Spoon, drizzle or spread icing over cooled cupcakes.

Maple Buttercream

*This buttercream has a light
maple flavor and is the
perfect partner for many
of my spiced cupcakes,
such as Pumpkin Cupcakes
(page 98), Carrot Zucchini
Cupcakes (page 117),
Applesauce Cupcakes
(page 102) or Spice
Cupcakes (page 99).*

Tip

Transfer frosting to an
airtight container and
refrigerate until ready to
use or for up to 2 days.
Before using, let stand at
room temperature until
soft enough to spread. Stir
until smooth.

2 cups	confectioner's (icing) sugar	500 mL
¾ cup	unsalted butter, at room temperature	175 mL
2 tbsp	pure maple syrup	30 mL
½ tsp	maple-flavored extract	2 mL
Pinch	salt	Pinch

1. In a bowl, using an electric mixer, beat together confectioner's sugar, butter, maple syrup, maple extract and salt until smooth.

2. Spread frosting over cooled cupcakes and set aside at room temperature until ready to serve or for up to 8 hours.

Orange Cream Cheese Icing

As I was developing recipes for this book, I realized that I had to have an orange cream cheese icing. The orange flavor is a great complement to many of the cupcake flavors in this book.

Tip

Transfer frosting to an airtight container and refrigerate until ready to use or for up to 2 days.

4 oz	cream cheese, at room temperature	125 g
1/2 cup	unsalted butter, at room temperature	125 mL
Pinch	salt	Pinch
2 1/2 cups	confectioner's (icing) sugar, sifted	625 mL
2 tsp	grated orange zest	10 mL
2 tsp	orange-flavored liqueur	10 mL

1. In a bowl, using an electric mixer on medium-high speed, beat together cream cheese, butter and salt until creamy. With mixer on low speed, beat in confectioner's sugar, 1/2 cup (125 mL) at a time so that the sugar doesn't fly all over the place. Increase speed to medium-high, beating until light and fluffy. Add orange zest and liqueur, beating until mixed.

2. This frosting is on the soft side, so before frosting cupcakes, refrigerate it for 30 to 60 minutes to firm it up. Spread frosting over cooled cupcakes and refrigerate until ready to serve or for up to 1 day.

Peanut Butter Frosting

Peanut butter makes a delicate and deliciously rich frosting, not to mention an absolutely divine addition to chocolate and vanilla cupcakes (or, of course, peanut butter cupcakes). This one is always a hit with the kids.

Tips

Store frosting in an airtight container and refrigerate until ready to use or for up to 2 days. Let soften at room temperature before using.

This frosting can be prepared in a food processor with excellent results.

Regular peanut butter rather than natural-style peanut butter works best in this recipe.

2 cups	confectioner's (icing) sugar	500 mL
½ cup	unsalted butter, at room temperature	125 mL
Pinch	salt	Pinch
½ cup	creamy peanut butter	125 mL
2 tbsp	milk	30 mL

1. In a bowl, using an electric mixer, beat together confectioner's sugar, butter and salt until creamy. Add peanut butter, beating well. Add milk and beat until smooth and creamy.

2. Spread frosting on cooled cupcakes.

Peanut Butter Fudge Frosting

Here's a frosting that's almost like candy. You've got your chocolate fudge and your peanut butter, blended together into an outstanding topping for chocolate cupcakes (or peanut butter cupcakes). It's delicious on almost anything.

Tips

Store frosting in an airtight container and refrigerate until ready to use or for up to 2 days. Let soften at room temperature before using.

Regular peanut butter rather than natural-style peanut butter works best in this recipe.

Variation

Use crunchy peanut butter instead of creamy.

¾ cup	unsalted butter, at room temperature	175 mL
½ cup	creamy peanut butter	125 mL
Pinch	salt	Pinch
2 cups	confectioner's (icing) sugar	500 mL
¾ cup	unsweetened Dutch-process cocoa powder, sifted	175 mL

1. In a bowl, beat together butter, peanut butter and salt until creamy. With mixer on low speed, beat in confectioner's sugar, ½ cup (125 mL) at a time so that the sugar doesn't fly all over the place. Add cocoa powder, beating until very smooth and creamy.

2. Spread frosting on cooled cupcakes.

Rum Buttercream

Smooth and silky with the rich flavor of rum, this buttercream will surely make you happy. With each bite, you'll feel transported to a breezy and tropical place (think blue water and white sandy beaches).

Tip

Store frosting in an airtight container and refrigerate until ready to use or for up to 2 days. Let soften at room temperature until spreading consistency before using.

Variation

Substitute coconut rum for the dark rum.

2 cups	confectioner's (icing) sugar	500 mL
½ cup	unsalted butter, at room temperature	125 mL
¼ cup	sour cream	60 mL
Pinch	salt	Pinch
1 tbsp	dark rum	15 mL

1. In a bowl, using an electric mixer, beat together confectioner's sugar, butter, sour cream and salt until smooth. Add rum, beating until smooth.

2. Spread frosting over cooled cupcakes and refrigerate until ready to serve or for up to 8 hours.

Strawberry Cream Cheese Buttercream

Makes about 2 cups (500 mL), enough to frost 16 cupcakes

Here's a pretty-in-pink frosting that tastes great, without adding any food coloring. This sweet frosting is a favorite with children, who tend to devour it before you're able to put it on the cupcakes.

Tip

Store frosting in an airtight container and refrigerate until ready to use or for up to 4 days. Let soften at room temperature before using.

Variation

Omit the lemon zest or substitute orange or lime zest.

4 oz	cream cheese, at room temperature	125 g
¼ cup	unsalted butter, at room temperature	60 mL
Pinch	salt	Pinch
2½ cups	confectioner's (icing) sugar	625 mL
⅓ cup	strawberry jam	75 mL
1 tsp	grated lemon zest	5 mL

1. In a bowl, using an electric mixer on medium-high speed, beat together cream cheese, butter and salt until creamy. With mixer on low speed, beat in confectioner's sugar, ½ cup (125 mL) at a time so that the sugar doesn't fly all over the place. Increase speed to medium-high and beat until light and fluffy. Beat in strawberry jam and lemon zest.

2. Spread frosting over cooled cupcakes and refrigerate until ready to serve.

Vanilla Ice Cream

Makes 6 cups (1.5 L)

When I need a fabulous, creamy, not-too-sweet vanilla ice cream, I make this recipe. One taste of this delicious ice cream and I am immediately transported back to my childhood birthday parties, at which we all took turns cranking the manual ice cream maker.

Tip

Store ice cream in the freezer for up to 1 day in an airtight container with a piece of plastic wrap pressed onto the surface. Homemade ice cream is best the day that it's made.

Variations

For a chocolate chip version, add ½ cup (125 mL) miniature semisweet chocolate chips during the last 5 minutes of freezing. For a fruit version, try adding 1 cup (250 mL) chopped pitted peeled fresh peaches or nectarines, or coarsely chopped strawberries, during the last 5 minutes of freezing.

• **Ice cream maker**

1½ cups	whipping (35%) cream	375 mL
1½ cups	milk	375 mL
½ cup	superfine sugar (see Tips, page 64)	125 mL
1 tsp	vanilla paste or extract (see Tip, page 28)	5 mL

1. In a bowl, whisk together cream, milk, sugar and vanilla paste until sugar is dissolved.

2. Pour mixture into an ice cream maker and freeze according to manufacturer's directions. Serve immediately or freeze in an airtight container (see Tip, left). Garnish cupcakes with a scoop or swirl of ice cream.

Vanilla Custard Filling

Although it takes a little extra effort, a creamy custard filling is a fun and delicious way to jazz up cupcakes. This custard is so good that my daughter likes to eat it with a spoon.

1/3 cup	granulated sugar	75 mL
1/4 cup	cornstarch	60 mL
Pinch	salt	Pinch
4	egg yolks	4
1 cup	milk	250 mL
1/2 cup	whipping (35%) cream	125 mL
1 tbsp	unsalted butter	15 mL
1 tsp	vanilla paste or vanilla (see Tip, page 28)	5 mL
1/3 cup	whipping (35%) cream	75 mL

1. In a heavy saucepan, whisk together sugar, cornstarch and salt. Whisk in egg yolks, milk and 1/2 cup (125 mL) whipping cream until smooth. Bring mixture to a simmer over medium heat, whisking constantly. Remove from heat and continue whisking until very thick. Whisk in butter and vanilla paste until butter is melted. Spoon pudding into a small bowl.

2. Fill a slightly larger bowl with ice. Place small bowl of custard on top of ice. Whisk custard until cool. Remove small bowl, dry bottom and sides with a towel so that no moisture touches custard. Whisk in 1/3 cup (75 mL) whipping cream.

3. Place a piece of plastic wrap on surface of custard and refrigerate until ready to use. It is best used the same day that it is made. Stir custard until smooth before using.

Whipped Cream Topping

A cloudlike topping of whipped cream is another fun way to top your cupcakes. You can alter the flavor of the whipped cream by using different flavored coffee syrups.

Tip

Sprinkle fresh berries or sliced almonds over whipped cream.

1 cup	whipping (35%) cream	250 mL
¼ cup	confectioner's (icing) sugar	60 mL
2 tbsp	almond-flavored syrup	30 mL

1. In a bowl, using an electric mixer, whip together cream, confectioner's sugar and almond syrup until stiff peaks form. Do not overbeat.

2. Just before serving, spread or dollop whipped topping over tops of cupcakes.

Vegan Chocolate Icing

Here's a great chocolate glaze that offers the special bonus of being fat-free. I love the sweet, rich, chocolaty flavor.

Tip

This icing cannot be made ahead of time, because it will harden and crack. Make it right before you're ready to use it.

1½ cups	confectioner's (icing) sugar	375 mL
½ cup	unsweetened Dutch-process cocoa powder, sifted	125 mL
3 tbsp	strong brewed coffee, at room temperature (approx.)	45 mL

1. In a bowl, whisk together confectioner's sugar and cocoa powder. Add coffee, whisking until smooth. If you prefer a slightly thinner icing to drizzle, rather than spread, over cupcakes, you can add 1 to 2 tsp (5 to 10 mL) more coffee.

2. Spoon, spread or drizzle icing over cooled cupcakes.

Vegan Chocolate Fudge Frosting

Makes about 1¾ cups (425 mL), enough to frost 12 cupcakes

This is my "go to" chocolate frosting. If you're looking for a frosting with a deep chocolate flavor, this is your frosting. It's thick and rich, perfect to spread on almost any cupcake flavor. Plus, this frosting is delicious eaten right off a spoon!

Tip

Store any unused frosting in an airtight container in the refrigerator. Let come to room temperature before using.

Variation

For a mocha version, substitute cooled strong-brewed coffee for the soy milk.

3 cups	confectioner's (icing) sugar	750 mL
1 cup	unsweetened Dutch-process cocoa powder, sifted	250 mL
½ cup	unhydrogenated vegan margarine, softened	125 mL
6 to 8 tbsp	vanilla soy milk (approx.)	90 to 125 mL
2 tsp	vanilla	10 mL

1. In a bowl, using a hand mixer or stand mixer on low speed, beat together confectioners' sugar, cocoa powder, margarine, 6 tbsp (90 mL) of the soy milk and vanilla until well combined. Gradually increase speed to high, adding additional 1 tbsp (15 mL) of soy milk, or more as needed to make a soft and fluffy frosting and beating until frosting is smooth.

Vegan Fluffy Almond Cream Frosting

Makes about 2½ cups (625 mL), enough to frost 12 cupcakes

This is a fabulous frosting. It's super fluffy, creamy and just sweet enough to top a cupcake. In order to get a super fluffy creamy texture, you really need a stand mixer with a whip attachment because it whips a lot of air into the frosting.

Tip

I have used the Spectrum brand of shortening and Whole Foods brand and both work great! If you don't have access to organic shortening, no worries.

1 cup	organic palm shortening, at room temperature (see Tip, left)	250 mL
3 cups	confectioner's (icing) sugar	750 mL
¼ cup	soy milk	60 mL
1 tsp	almond extract	5 mL

1. In bowl of a stand mixer fitted with whisk attachment, combine shortening, confectioner's sugar, soy milk and almond extract.

2. With mixer on low, slowly whip ingredients until blended and confectioner's sugar is incorporated. Stop machine and scrape sides of bowl with a spatula. Increase speed to high and whip frosting mixture until super fluffy and has the texture of mousse, about 5 minutes, depending on your mixer.

3. Scoop frosting into a pastry bag and pipe on cooled cupcakes. Alternatively, use an offset spatula or the back of a spoon to swirl the frosting decoratively onto the cooled cupcakes.

Vegan Fluffy Lemon Cream Frosting

Makes about 2½ cups (625 mL), enough to frost 12 cupcakes

I could eat this frosting with a spoon! It's got a wonderful light and creamy texture, which goes really well with lemon or vanilla cupcakes.

Variation

For an orange version, substitute ½ to ¾ tsp (2 to 3 mL) or to taste, of pure orange oil. My favorite citrus oils are from Boyajian (see Sources, page 185).

1 cup	organic palm shortening, at room temperature (see Tip, page 178)	250 mL
3 cups	confectioner's (icing) sugar	750 mL
¼ cup	soy milk	60 mL
1 tsp	pure lemon oil	5 mL
	Small drop of yellow food coloring, optional	

1. In bowl of a stand mixer fitted with whisk attachment, combine shortening, confectioner's sugar, soy milk and lemon oil.

2. With mixer on low, slowly whip ingredients until blended and confectioner's sugar is incorporated. Stop machine and scrape sides of bowl with a spatula. If desired, add a tiny drop of yellow food coloring. Increase speed to high and whip frosting mixture until super fluffy and has the texture of mousse, about 5 minutes, depending on your mixer.

3. Scoop frosting into a pastry bag and pipe on cooled cupcakes. Alternatively, use an offset spatula or the back of a spoon to swirl the frosting decoratively onto the cooled cupcakes.

Vegan Large Batch Fluffy Frosting

1¹⁄₂ cups	organic palm shortening, room temperature (see Tip, page 178)	375 mL
4¹⁄₂ cups	confectioner's (icing) sugar	1.125 L
6 tbsp	vanilla or plain soy milk	90 mL
1 tbsp	vanilla paste or extract (see Tip, page 28)	15 mL

There are a couple of things that are super important here to get a super fluffy creamy texture. The first is using a stand mixer with a whip attachment because it whips a lot of air into the frosting. The second is using organic palm shortening. Something about it whips into the creamiest texture.

Tip

Although this seems like a big recipe, it's perfect if you're frosting a lot of cupcakes, or want to pipe a generous amount of frosting on each cupcake. I use this recipe when I frost cupcakes for our food cart. Customers love lots of frosting!

1. In bowl of a stand mixer fitted with whisk attachment, combine shortening, confectioner's sugar, soy milk and vanilla.

2. With mixer on low, slowly whip ingredients until blended and confectioner's sugar is incorporated. Stop machine and scrape sides of bowl with a spatula. Increase speed to high and whip frosting mixture until it's super light and fluffy and has the texture of mousse, about 5 minutes, depending on your mixer.

3. Scoop frosting into a pastry bag and pipe on cooled cupcakes. Alternatively, use an offset spatula or the back of a spoon to swirl the frosting decoratively onto the cooled cupcakes.

Vegan Lemon Glaze

Tangy and tart, this lemon glaze is easy to make. The lemon zest kicks up the flavor of the cupcake and offers an elegant-looking garnish.

Tips

If you prefer a thinner glaze, you can add an additional teaspoon (5 mL) or so of lemon juice.

This icing cannot be made ahead of time because it hardens quickly. Make right before you're ready to use it.

Variation

Substitute lime zest and juice for the lemon zest and juice.

2 cups	confectioner's (icing) sugar	500 mL
1 tsp	grated lemon zest	5 mL
3 tbsp	freshly squeezed lemon juice	45 mL

1. In a bowl, using an electric mixer, beat together confectioner's sugar, and lemon zest and juice until smooth.

2. Drizzle or spread icing over cooled cupcakes.

Vegan Peanut Butter Frosting

Makes about 1¾ cups (425 mL), enough to frost 12 cupcakes

This frosting is super good and it's all I can do not to frost everything in my kitchen with it. Of course it's best on homemade cupcakes, but you could always spread a little on chocolate cookies, too. Don't worry, I won't tell.

Tips

Use natural peanut butter for this recipe.

Try this frosting on any of the chocolate or vanilla cupcakes, although it would be fabulous on banana cupcakes, too.

Variation

For a nuttier version, use chunky peanut butter.

2¼ cups	confectioner's (icing) sugar	550 mL
½ cup	smooth or creamy peanut butter	125 mL
¼ cup	non-dairy, non-hydrogenated margarine, softened	60 mL
4 to 5 tbsp	plain or vanilla soy milk	60 to 75 mL
1 tsp	vanilla	5 mL

1. In bowl of stand mixer, combine confectioner's sugar, peanut butter, margarine, soy milk and vanilla.

2. With mixer on low, slowly whip ingredients until blended and confectioner's sugar is incorporated. Increase speed to high and whip frosting until light and fluffy, about 5 minutes, depending on your mixer. Use right away or refrigerate for up to 1 week until ready to use. Let frosting stand at room temperature to soften to spreading consistency before using.

Vegan Fluffy Vanilla Cream Frosting

Makes about 2 cups (500 mL), enough to frost 12 cupcakes

This is a perfect plain Jane frosting to offset some of the bold flavors of cupcakes in this book. I mean plain Jane in the most positive way; it's got a subtle flavor and is perfectly sweet and not overpowering with it's own bold flavors.

Tips

There are a couple of things that are super important here to get a super fluffy creamy texture. The first is using a stand mixer with a whip attachment because it whips a lot of air into the frosting. The second is using organic palm shortening. Something about it whips into the creamiest texture.

This frosting will work with all shortenings, but it seems to work best with the organic palm shortening.

1 cup	organic palm shortening, at room temperature (see Tips, left)	250 mL
3 cups	confectioner's (icing) sugar	750 mL
¼ cup	vanilla or plain soy milk	60 mL
1 tbsp	vanilla paste or extract (see Tip, page 28)	15 mL

1. In bowl of a stand mixer fitted with whisk attachment, combine shortening, confectioner's sugar, soy milk and vanilla.

2. With mixer on low, slowly whip ingredients until blended and confectioner's sugar is incorporated. Stop machine and scrape sides of bowl with a spatula. Increase speed to high and whip frosting mixture until it's super fluffy and has the texture of mousse, about 5 minutes, depending on your mixer.

3. Scoop frosting into a pastry bag and pipe on cooled cupcakes. Alternatively, use an offset spatula or the back of a spoon to swirl the frosting decoratively onto the cooled cupcakes.

Vegan Cream Cheese Frosting

Makes about 1⅔ cups (400 mL), enough to frost 12 cupcakes

3 cups	confectioner's (icing) sugar	750 mL
½ cup	non-dairy cream cheese	125 mL
¼ cup	non-dairy, non-hydrogenated margarine, softened	60 mL

This frosting is the bomb! It's creamy and decadent and no one would ever guess that it's vegan. Plus, you get the added benefit of knowing that it's cholesterol and cruelty free and requires just three ingredients.

Tips

This frosting whips up best in a stand mixer.

Frosting will keep refrigerated and in an airtight container for about 1 week.

I think that this frosting is perfect and goes on just about every cupcake in this book.

1. In bowl of stand mixer, combine confectioner's sugar, cream cheese and margarine.

2. With mixer on low, slowly whip ingredients until blended and confectioner's sugar is incorporated. Increase speed to high and whip frosting until light and fluffy. Use right away or refrigerate until ready to use. Let frosting sit out to soften to spreading consistency before using.

Sources

Boyajian
(800) 965-0665
www.boyajianinc.com
Citrus oils and flavorings.

Charles H. Baldwin & Sons
(413) 232-7785
www.baldwinextracts.com
Pure extracts, from anise to peppermint.

Demarle at Home
(888) 838-1998 or (248) 684-1480
www.demarleathome.com
Silpat® pan liners, silicone baking
pans and specialty cookware.

Golda's Kitchen
(866) 465-3299
www.goldaskitchen.com
Quality kitchenware products, including
specialty cake decorating, chocolate and
confectionery supplies.

Julie Hasson
www.juliehasson.com
www.everydaydish.tv
Author's websites with recipes and online
cooking show.

King Arthur Flour
(800) 827-6836
www.kingarthurflour.com
An amazing selection of baking
and cooking tools, specialty flours,
chocolates, hard-to-find ingredients,
sprinkles, colored sugars and more.

Qualifirst
(416) 244-1177
www.qualifirst.com
Canadian distributor for Boyajian,
including citrus oils. Also fine chocolate
and much more.

Surfas
(310) 559-4770
www.surfasonline.com
Restaurant supply and gourmet food.

Sur La Table
(800) 243-0852
www.surlatable.com
Specialty bakeware, cookware, utensils
and chocolate.

Williams-Sonoma
(877) 812-6235 (U.S.)
(866) 753-1350 (Canada)
www.williams-sonoma.com
www.williams-sonoma.ca
Specialty bakeware, cookware, utensils and
specialty gourmet food.

Wilton
(800) 794-5866 (U.S.)
(800) 387-3300 (Canada)
www.wilton.com
Bakeware, decorating supplies, food
coloring and sprinkles.

Library and Archives Canada Cataloguing in Publication

Hasson, Julie
    150 best cupcake recipes / Julie Hasson.

Includes index.
ISBN 978-0-7788-0290-7

    1. Cupcakes. 2. Cookbooks. I. Title. II. Title: One hundred fifty best cupcake recipes.

TX771.H375 2012   641.86'53   C2011-907445-1

Index

(v) = variation

A

Almonds
  almond meal, 23
  Almond Poppy Seed Cupcakes,
    49
  Anise Cupcakes (v), 90
  Awesome Almond Cupcakes, 50
  Butterscotch Chocolate
    Coconut Cupcakes (v), 27
  Flourless Chocolate Cupcakes,
    23
  Vegan Cinnamon Almond
    Cupcakes (v), 136
  Whipped Cream Frosting (v),
    175
Anise Cupcakes, 90
Apple Crisp Cupcakes, 30
Applesauce Cupcakes, 102
Apricots
  Apricot Rum Cupcakes, 31
  Apricot Spice Cupcakes, 32
  Blueberry Apricot Cupcakes, 33
  Princess Cupcakes, 120
  Raspberry Vanilla Cupcakes
    (v), 107
  Sherry Apricot Cupcakes, 66
Awesome Almond Cupcakes, 50

B

Bananas
  Banana Cupcakes, 44
  Banana Nutmeg Cupcakes, 91
Best Chocolate Cupcakes, 18
Blueberries
  Blueberry Apricot Cupcakes, 33
  Blueberry Rose Cupcakes, 42
Boston Cream Cupcakes, 122
Butter, about, 13
Buttercream Frosting, 159
  White Cupcakes with Coconut
    Frosting (v), 116
Buttermilk, about, 13
  Almond Poppy Seed Cupcakes,
    49
  Applesauce Cupcakes, 102
  Apricot Rum Cupcakes, 31
  Best Chocolate Cupcakes, 18
  Candied Pecan Cupcakes, 48
  Candy Bar Cupcakes, 76
  Chai Cupcakes, 104
  Chocolate Chile Cupcakes, 94
  Chocolate Gingerbread
    Cupcakes, 20
  Chocolate Surprise Cupcakes, 22
  Coconut Cupcakes, 82

Confetti Cupcakes, 79
Earl Grey Cupcakes, 73
Green Tea Cupcakes, 74
Kahlúa Cupcakes, 63
Lamington Cupcakes, 108
Lemon Buttermilk Cupcakes,
  46
Orange Date Cupcakes, 39
Peanut Butter and Jelly
  Cupcakes, 52
Peppermint Candy Cupcakes,
  83
Piña Colada Cupcakes, 40
Pink Lemonade Cupcakes, 88
Pretty in Pink Cupcakes, 87
Princess Cupcakes, 120
Sherry Apricot Cupcakes, 66
S'more Cupcakes, 110
Spice Cupcakes, 99
Toasted Sesame Cupcakes, 118
Toffee Cupcakes, 84
Tropical Cupcakes, 43
Vanilla Peanut Butter Cup
  Cupcakes, 54
White Chocolate Chip
  Cupcakes, 26
White Cupcakes, 85
Butterscotch Chocolate Coconut
  Cupcakes, 27

C

Candied Pecan Cupcakes, 48
Candy
  Candy Bar Cupcakes, 76
  Peppermint Candy Cupcakes,
    83
Cappuccino Cupcakes, 69
Caramel Frosting, 148
  Applesauce Cupcakes, 102
  Apple Crisp Cupcakes, 30
  Apricot Spice Cupcakes, 32
  Banana Cupcakes, 44
  Candied Pecan Cupcakes, 48
  Candy Bar Cupcakes, 76
  Carrot Cupcakes, 93
  Carrot Zucchini Cupcakes, 117
  Chai Cupcakes, 104
  Earl Grey Cupcakes, 73
  Ginger Cupcakes, 96
  Pumpkin Cupcakes, 98
  Rum Raisin Cupcakes, 67
  Sherry Apricot Cupcakes, 66
  Spiced Peach Cupcakes, 101
  Toffee Cupcakes, 84
Cardamom Plum Cupcakes, 92
Carrots
  Carrot Cupcakes, 93
  Carrot Zucchini Cupcakes, 117

Vegan Carrot Raisin Cupcakes,
  129
Cassis Cupcakes, 62
Chai Cupcakes, 104
Cheesecake Cupcakes, 112
Cherries
  Almond Poppy Seed Cupcakes
    (v), 49
  Cherry Almond Poppy Seed
    Cupcakes, 34
  Hot Fudge Sauce (v), 163
  Raspberry Vanilla Cupcakes
    (v), 107
  Rum Raisin Cupcakes (v), 67
  Vegan Cherry Almond
    Cupcakes, 130
  Vegan Chocolate Cherry
    Cupcakes, 126
  Vegan Chocolate Cupcakes (v),
    131
Chile powder, Chocolate Chile
  Cupcakes, 94
Chocolate, about, 12. See also
  Chocolate chips; Cocoa
  powder
  Banana Nutmeg Cupcakes (v),
    91
  Boston Cream Cupcakes, 122
  Chocolate Cheesecake
    Cupcakes, 114
  Chocolate Glaze (v), 150
  Chocolate Surprise Cupcakes,
    22
  Chocolate Toffee Sauce, 153
  Cookies and Cream
    Buttercream, 157
  Cookies and Cream Cupcakes,
    77
  Espresso Dark Brownie
    Cupcakes, 72
  Flourless Chocolate Cupcakes,
    23
  Peanut Butter Cupcakes (v), 51
  S'more Cupcakes, 110
  Sticky Date Cupcakes (v), 119
  Vanilla Peanut Butter Cup
    Cupcakes, 54
Chocolate chips
  Awesome Almond Cupcakes
    (v), 50
  Banana Cupcakes (v), 44
  Best Chocolate Cupcakes, 18
  Butterscotch Chocolate
    Coconut Cupcakes, 27
  Cappuccino Cupcakes, 69
  Cheesecake Cupcakes (v), 112
  Chocolate Brownie Cupcakes,
    24
  Chocolate Chile Cupcakes, 94

Chocolate Chip Cookie
  Cupcakes, 106
Chocolate Chip Cream Cheese
  Cupcakes, 109
Chocolate Gingerbread
  Cupcakes, 20
Chocolate Glaze, 150
Chocolate Mint Cupcakes, 86
Chocolate Mousse Filling, 151
Chocolate Peanut Butter
  Cupcakes, 19
Coconut Cupcakes (v), 82
Coconut Pecan Frosting, 154
Coffee Ice Cream (v), 156
Crème de Menthe Cupcakes, 61
Hazelnut Chocolate Cupcakes,
  56
Jay's Favorite Chocolate
  Cupcakes, 70
Lamington Cupcakes, 108
Mocha Cupcakes (v), 71
Orange Chocolate Cupcakes, 25
Orange Date Cupcakes (v), 39
Orange-Scented Angel Food
  Cupcakes, 124
Peppermint Candy Cupcakes
  (v), 83
S'more Cupcakes, 110
Spice Cupcakes (v), 99
Toffee Cupcakes (v), 84
Vanilla Ice Cream (v), 173
Vegan Cherry Almond
  Cupcakes (v), 130
Vegan Chocolate Cherry
  Cupcakes (v), 126
Vegan Chocolate Cinnamon
  Cupcakes, 127
Vegan Chocolate Orange
  Cupcakes, 132
Vegan Chocolate Raspberry
  Cupcakes, 135
Vegan Coffee Cupcakes (v),
  138
Vegan Mocha Cupcakes, 142
Very Vanilla Chocolate Chip
  Cupcakes, 28
White Chocolate Macadamia
  Cupcakes (v), 58
Zucchini Chocolate Spice
  Cupcakes, 100
Chocolate Fudge Frosting, 149
Almond Poppy Seed Cupcakes,
  49
Awesome Almond Cupcakes,
  50
Banana Cupcakes, 44
Banana Nutmeg Cupcakes, 91
Best Chocolate Cupcakes, 18
Butterscotch Chocolate
  Coconut Cupcakes, 27
Candy Bar Cupcakes, 76
Cappuccino Cupcakes, 69
Chocolate Brownie Cupcakes,
  24

Chocolate Chile Cupcakes, 94
Chocolate Chip Cookie
  Cupcakes, 106
Chocolate Chip Cream Cheese
  Cupcakes, 109
Chocolate Gingerbread
  Cupcakes, 20
Chocolate Mint Cupcakes, 86
Chocolate Peanut Butter
  Cupcakes, 19
Chocolate Raspberry Cupcakes,
  21
Chocolate Surprise Cupcakes,
  22
Coconut Cupcakes, 82
Cookies and Cream Cupcakes,
  77
Crème de Menthe Cupcakes, 61
Espresso Dark Brownie
  Cupcakes, 72
Hazelnut Chocolate Cupcakes,
  56
Jay's Favorite Chocolate
  Cupcakes, 70
Kahlúa Cupcakes, 63
Madeleine Cupcakes, 121
Malted Milk Cupcakes, 80
Mocha Cupcakes, 71
Orange Chocolate Cupcakes,
  25
Peanut Butter Chip Cupcakes,
  53
Peppermint Candy Cupcakes,
  83
Toffee Cupcakes, 84
Vanilla Peanut Butter Cup
  Cupcakes, 54
Very Vanilla Chocolate Chip
  Cupcakes, 28
White Cupcakes, 85
Zucchini Chocolate Spice
  Cupcakes, 100
Chocolate Glaze, 150
Chocolate Chile Cupcakes, 94
Chocolate Chip Cookie
  Cupcakes, 106
Chocolate Mint Cupcakes, 86
Chocolate Surprise Cupcakes,
  22
Crème de Menthe Cupcakes, 61
Raspberry Vanilla Cupcakes,
  107
White Cupcakes, 85
Zucchini Chocolate Spice
  Cupcakes, 100
Chocolate Hazelnut Frosting, 152
Hazelnut Chocolate Cupcakes,
  56
Chocolate Mousse Filling, 151
Kahlúa Cupcakes (v), 63
Chocolate Toffee Sauce, 153,
Sticky Date Cupcakes, 119
Cocoa powder, about, 12
Best Chocolate Cupcakes, 18

Candy Bar Cupcakes, 76
Chocolate Brownie Cupcakes,
  24
Chocolate Cheesecake
  Cupcakes, 114
Chocolate Chile Cupcakes, 94
Chocolate Fudge Frosting, 149
Chocolate Gingerbread
  Cupcakes, 20
Chocolate Hazelnut Frosting,
  152
Chocolate Mint Cupcakes, 86
Chocolate Peanut Butter
  Cupcakes, 19
Chocolate Raspberry Cupcakes,
  21
Espresso Dark Brownie
  Cupcakes, 72
Flourless Chocolate Cupcakes,
  23
Hot Fudge Sauce, 163
Jay's Favorite Chocolate
  Cupcakes, 70
Lamington Cupcakes, 108
Mocha Cupcakes, 71
Peanut Butter Fudge Frosting,
  170
S'more Cupcakes, 110
Vegan Chocolate Cherry
  Cupcakes, 126
Vegan Chocolate Cinnamon
  Cupcakes, 127
Vegan Chocolate Cupcakes,
  131
Vegan Chocolate Fudge
  Frosting, 177
Vegan Chocolate Icing, 176
Vegan Chocolate Orange
  Cupcakes, 132
Vegan Chocolate Peppermint
  Cupcakes, 134
Vegan Chocolate Raspberry
  Cupcakes, 135
Vegan Mocha Cupcakes, 142
Zucchini Chocolate Spice
  Cupcakes, 100
Coconut
  Butterscotch Chocolate
    Coconut Cupcakes, 27
  Carrot Cupcakes, 93
  Carrot Zucchini Cupcakes (v),
    117
  Coconut Cupcakes, 82
  Coconut Pecan Frosting, 154
  Lamington Cupcakes, 108
  Mango Coconut Cupcakes, 37
  Piña Colada Cupcakes, 40
  toasting, 108
  Vegan Coconut Cupcakes (v),
    137
  White Cupcakes with Coconut
    Frosting, 116
Coconut milk
  Vegan Coconut Cupcakes, 137

Coconut Pecan Frosting, 154
  German Chocolate Cupcakes
    (v), 18
Coconut rum
  Rum Buttercream (v), 171
Coffee, about, 12
  Cappuccino Cupcakes, 69
  Chocolate Chile Cupcakes, 94
  Chocolate Fudge Frosting, 149
  Chocolate Mousse Filling, 151
  Coffee Buttercream, 155
  Coffee Ice Cream, 156
  Jay's Favorite Chocolate
    Cupcakes, 70
  Malted Espresso Cupcakes, 68
  Malted Milk Espresso Icing,
    166
  Mocha Cupcakes, 71
  Vegan Chocolate Cinnamon
    Cupcakes, 127
  Vegan Chocolate Fudge
    Frosting (v), 177
  Vegan Chocolate Icing, 176
  Vegan Coffee Cupcakes, 138
  Vegan Mocha Cupcakes, 142
Coffee Buttercream, 155
  Cappuccino Cupcakes, 69
  Chocolate Brownie Cupcakes,
    24
  Kahlúa Cupcakes, 63
  Malted Espresso Cupcakes, 68
  Mocha Cupcakes, 71
  White Chocolate Chip
    Cupcakes, 26
Coffee Ice Cream, 156
  Cappuccino Cupcakes, 69
  Chocolate Brownie Cupcakes,
    24
  Espresso Dark Brownie
    Cupcakes, 72
  Jay's Favorite Chocolate
    Cupcakes, 70
Confetti Cupcakes, 79
Cookies and Cream Buttercream,
  157
  Best Chocolate Cupcakes, 18
  Cookies and Cream Cupcakes,
    77
  White Cupcakes, 85
Cookies and Cream Cupcakes,
  77
Cranberries,
  Cherry Almond Poppy Seed
    Cupcakes (v), 34
  Cranberry Lemon Cupcakes, 35
Cream cheese, about, 13
  Cheesecake Cupcakes, 112
  Chocolate Cheesecake
    Cupcakes, 114
  Chocolate Chip Cream Cheese
    Cupcakes, 109
  Cream Cheese Icing, 158
  Ginger Cream Cheese Icing,
    161

Honey Cream Cheese Frosting,
  162
Lemon Cheesecake Cupcakes,
  113
Orange Cream Cheese Icing,
  168
Strawberry Cream Cheese
  Buttercream, 172
Vegan Cream Cheese Frosting,
  184
Cream Cheese Icing, 158
  Almond Poppy Seed Cupcakes,
    49
  Anise Cupcakes, 90
  Apple Crisp Cupcakes, 30
  Applesauce Cupcakes, 102
  Apricot Spice Cupcakes, 32
  Banana Cupcakes, 44
  Banana Nutmeg Cupcakes, 91
  Best Chocolate Cupcakes, 18
  Carrot Cupcakes, 93
  Carrot Zucchini Cupcakes, 117
  Chai Cupcakes, 104
  Chocolate Raspberry Cupcakes,
    21
  Coconut Cupcakes, 82
  French Toast Cupcakes, 95
  Ginger Cupcakes, 96
  Mango Coconut Cupcakes, 37
  Orange Date Cupcakes, 39
  Piña Colada Cupcakes, 40
  Pineapple Cupcakes, 41
  Pink Lemonade Cupcakes, 88
  Pistachio Cupcakes, 55
  Pumpkin Cupcakes, 98
  Raspberry Vanilla Cupcakes,
    107
  Spice Cupcakes, 99
  White Chocolate Macadamia
    Cupcakes, 58
  White Cupcakes with Coconut
    Frosting, 116
  Zucchini Chocolate Spice
    Cupcakes, 100
Crème de Menthe Cupcakes, 61

D

Dates
  Figgy Cupcakes (v), 36
  Orange Date Cupcakes, 39
  Sticky Date Cupcakes, 119
Decorating, 9
Decorating equipment, 12
Dried fruit, about, 13

E

Earl Grey Cupcakes, 73
Easy Buttercream Frosting, 159
  Anise Cupcakes, 90
  Banana Nutmeg Cupcakes, 91
  Blueberry Apricot Cupcakes,
    33

Boston Cream Cupcakes (v),
  122
Cardamom Plum Cupcakes, 92
Cherry Almond Poppy Seed
  Cupcakes, 34
Confetti Cupcakes, 79
Cranberry Lemon Cupcakes, 35
Green Tea Cupcakes, 74
Lemon Buttermilk Cupcakes,
  46
Madeleine Cupcakes, 121
Margarita Cupcakes, 64
Orange Date Cupcakes, 39
Peanut Butter Chip Cupcakes,
  53
Peppermint Candy Cupcakes,
  83
Pimm's Cupcakes, 60
Pink Lemonade Cupcakes, 88
Pistachio Cupcakes, 55
Pretty in Pink Cupcakes, 87
Princess Cupcakes, 120
Spiced Peach Cupcakes, 101
Toasted Sesame Cupcakes, 118
Toffee Cupcakes, 84
Very Vanilla Chocolate Chip
  Cupcakes, 28
Easy Butterscotch Frosting, 159
  Awesome Almond Cupcakes,
    50
  Cassis Cupcakes, 62
  Nectarine Cupcakes, 38
Eggs, about, 13
Espresso Dark Brownie
  Cupcakes, 72
Extracts, about, 13

F

Figgy Cupcakes, 36
Fillings. See also Glazes; Sauces;
  Toppings
  Chocolate Mousse Filling, 151
  Lemon Curd, 165
  Vanilla Custard Filling, 174
Flavorings, about, 13
Flour, about, 13
Flourless Chocolate Cupcakes, 23
French Toast Cupcakes, 95
Frostings. See also Fillings;
  Glazes; Sauces; Toppings
  Caramel Frosting, 148
  Chocolate Fudge Frosting, 149
  Chocolate Hazelnut Frosting,
    152
  Coconut Pecan Frosting, 154
  Cookies and Cream
    Buttercream, 157
  Cream Cheese Icing, 158
  Easy Buttercream Frosting, 159
  Ginger Cream Cheese Icing,
    161
  Honey Cream Cheese Frosting,
    162

Malted Milk Espresso Icing, 166
Maple Buttercream, 167
Orange Cream Cheese Icing, 168
Peanut Butter Frosting, 169
Peanut Butter Fudge Frosting, 170
Rum Buttercream, 171
Strawberry Cream Cheese Buttercream, 172
Vanilla Cream Frosting, 160
Vegan Chocolate Fudge Frosting, 177
Vegan Chocolate Icing, 176
Vegan Cream Cheese Frosting, 184
Vegan Fluffy Almond Cream Frosting, 178
Vegan Fluffy Lemon Cream Frosting, 179
Vegan Fluffy Vanilla Cream Frosting, 183
Vegan Large Batch Frosting, 180
Vegan Peanut Butter Frosting, 182
Whipped Cream Frosting, 175
Fruit. See also individual varieties
Apple Crisp Cupcakes, 30
Apricot Rum Cupcakes, 31
Apricot Spice Cupcakes, 32
Banana Cupcakes, 44
Banana Nutmeg Cupcakes, 91
Blueberry Apricot Cupcakes, 33
Blueberry Rose Cupcakes, 42
Cardamom Plum Cupcakes, 92
Cherry Almond Poppy Seed Cupcakes, 34
Cranberry Lemon Cupcakes, 35
Figgy Cupcakes, 36
Lemon Buttermilk Cupcakes, 46
Lemon Yogurt Cupcakes, 45
Mango Coconut Cupcakes, 37
Nectarine Cupcakes, 38
Orange Date Cupcakes, 39
Piña Colada Cupcakes, 40
Pineapple Cupcakes, 41
Raspberry Vanilla Cupcakes, 107
Spiced Peach Cupcakes, 101
Tropical Cupcakes, 43
Vanilla Ice Cream (v), 173
Vegan Chocolate Raspberry Cupcakes, 135
Whipped Cream Frosting (v), 175

G

Garnishes, 10
German Chocolate Cupcakes (v), 18

Ginger
Chocolate Gingerbread Cupcakes, 20
Ginger Cream Cheese Icing, 161
Ginger Cupcakes, 96
Ginger Cream Cheese Icing, 161
Apricot Spice Cupcakes, 32
Carrot Cupcakes, 93
Chocolate Gingerbread Cupcakes, 20
Figgy Cupcakes, 36
Ginger Cupcakes, 96
Lemon Buttermilk Cupcakes, 46
Mango Coconut Cupcakes, 37
Spice Cupcakes, 99
Tropical Cupcakes, 43
Glazes. See also Fillings; Sauces; Toppings
Chocolate Glaze, 150
Vegan Lemon Glaze, 181
Green Tea Cupcakes, 74

H

Hazelnut Chocolate Cupcakes, 56
Hazelnut meal, 56
Hazelnut spread
Chocolate Hazelnut Frosting, 152
Homemade Marshmallows, 15
Honey Cream Cheese Frosting, 162
Blueberry Apricot Cupcakes, 33
Cardamom Plum Cupcakes, 92
Nectarine Cupcakes, 38
Spiced Peach Cupcakes, 101
Hot Fudge Sauce, 163
Cappuccino Cupcakes, 69
Chocolate Chip Cookie Cupcakes, 106
Jay's Favorite Chocolate Cupcakes, 70
Pistachio Cupcakes (v), 55

I

Ice cream
Coffee Ice Cream, 156
Cookies and Cream Cupcakes (v), 77
Vanilla Ice Cream, 173
Ice Cream Cone Cupcakes, 78
Icing. See Frostings

J

Jam
Peanut Butter and Jelly Cupcakes, 52
Raspberry Vanilla Cupcakes, 107

Strawberry Cream Cheese Buttercream, 172
Vegan Chocolate Cupcakes (v), 131
Jay's Favorite Chocolate Cupcakes, 70

K

Kahlúa Cupcakes, 63

L

Lamington Cupcakes, 108
Lemon
Cranberry Lemon Cupcakes, 35
Lemon Buttermilk Cupcakes, 46
Lemon Cheesecake Cupcakes, 113
Lemon Curd, 165
Lemon Yogurt Cupcakes, 45
Vegan Lemon Cupcakes, 141
Vegan Lemon Glaze, 181
Lemon Cream, 164
Lemon Buttermilk Cupcakes, 46
Lemon Yogurt Cupcakes, 45
Pimm's Cupcakes, 60
Raspberry Vanilla Cupcakes, 107
Lemon Curd, 165
Lemon Cheesecake Cupcakes, 113
Lemon Cream, 164
Lemon oil, about, 13
Cranberry Lemon Cupcakes, 35
Lemon Buttermilk Cupcakes, 46
Lemon Yogurt Cupcakes, 45
Madeleine Cupcakes (v), 121
Pimm's Cupcakes, 60
Vegan Fluffy Lemon Cream Frosting, 179
Vegan Lemon Cupcakes, 141
Lemonade, Pink Lemonade Cupcakes, 88
Lime
Lemon Curd (v), 165
Lemon Yogurt Cupcakes (v), 45
Margarita Cupcakes, 64
Vegan Lemon Glaze (v), 181
Lime oil
Margarita Cupcakes, 64
Liqueurs, about, 13
Chocolate Cheesecake Cupcakes, 114
Chocolate Fudge Frosting, 149
Chocolate Surprise Cupcakes, 22
Coffee Buttercream, 155
Margarita Cupcakes, 64

M

Macadamia nuts
  Chocolate Chip Cookie
    Cupcakes (v), 106
  Piña Colada Cupcakes (v), 40
  Tropical Cupcakes, 43
  White Chocolate Macadamia
    Cupcakes, 58
Madeleine Cupcakes, 121
Malted Espresso Cupcakes, 68
Malted Milk Cupcakes, 80
Malted Milk Espresso Icing, 166
  Malted Espresso Cupcakes, 68
  Malted Milk Cupcakes, 80
Malted milk powder, about, 68
  Malted Espresso Cupcakes, 68
  Malted Milk Cupcakes, 80
  Malted Milk Espresso Icing,
    166
Mangos
  Mango Coconut Cupcakes, 37
  Tropical Cupcakes, 43
Maple Buttercream, 167
  Applesauce Cupcakes, 102
  Candied Pecan Cupcakes, 48
  French Toast Cupcakes, 95
  Maple Raisin Cupcakes, 97
  Pumpkin Cupcakes, 98
  Spice Cupcakes, 99
Maple Raisin Cupcakes, 97
Margarita Cupcakes, 64
Marshmallow crème
  S'more Cupcakes, 110
Marshmallows
  Chocolate Surprise Cupcakes, 22
Marzipan
  Princess Cupcakes, 120
Matcha, about, 74
  Green Tea Cupcakes, 74
  Vegan Green Tea Matcha
    Cupcakes, 140
Mocha Cupcakes, 71

N

Nectarine Cupcakes, 38
Nuts, about, 14. See also
    individual varieties
  Almond Poppy Seed Cupcakes,
    49
  Awesome Almond Cupcakes,
    50
  Candied Pecan Cupcakes, 48
  Hazelnut Chocolate Cupcakes,
    56
  Peanut Butter and Jelly
    Cupcakes, 52
  Peanut Butter Chip Cupcakes,
    53
  Peanut Butter Cupcakes, 51
  Pistachio Cupcakes, 55
  Vanilla Peanut Butter Cup
    Cupcakes, 54

White Chocolate Macadamia
    Cupcakes, 58

O

Oil, about, 14
Orange
  Apricot Spice Cupcakes, 32
  Figgy Cupcakes, 36
  Madeleine Cupcakes, 121
  Orange Chocolate Cupcakes,
    25
  Orange Cream Cheese Icing,
    168
  Orange Date Cupcakes, 39
  Orange-Scented Angel Food
    Cupcakes, 124
  Vegan Chocolate Orange
    Cupcakes, 132
  Vegan Creamsicle Cupcakes,
    139
Orange Cream Cheese Icing, 168
  Almond Poppy Seed Cupcakes,
    49
  Carrot Zucchini Cupcakes, 117
  Earl Grey Cupcakes, 73
  Figgy Cupcakes, 36
  Jay's Favorite Chocolate
    Cupcakes, 70
  Madeleine Cupcakes, 121
  Orange Chocolate Cupcakes,
    25
  Orange Date Cupcakes, 39
  Very Vanilla Chocolate Chip
    Cupcakes, 28
Orange oil, about, 25
  Earl Grey Cupcakes, 73
  Orange Chocolate Cupcakes, 25
  Vegan Chocolate Orange
    Cupcakes, 132
  Vegan Creamsicle Cupcakes,
    139
  Vegan Fluffy Lemon Cream
    Frosting (v), 179
  Vegan Lemon Cupcakes (v),
    141
  Vegan Mocha Cupcakes, 142

P

Papaya
  Tropical Cupcakes, 43
Peaches
  Nectarine Cupcakes (v), 38
  Spiced Peach Cupcakes, 101
Peanut butter
  Chocolate Peanut Butter
    Cupcakes, 19
  Peanut Butter and Jelly
    Cupcakes, 52
  Peanut Butter Cupcakes, 51
  Peanut Butter Frosting, 169
  Peanut Butter Fudge Frosting,
    170

Vegan Peanut Butter Frosting,
    182
Peanut butter chips
  Chocolate Raspberry Cupcakes
    (v), 21
  Peanut Butter Chip Cupcakes,
    53
Peanut Butter Frosting, 169
  Candy Bar Cupcakes, 76
  Chocolate Peanut Butter
    Cupcakes, 19
  Chocolate Raspberry Cupcakes
    (v), 21
  Espresso Dark Brownie
    Cupcakes, 72
  Ice Cream Cone Cupcakes, 78
  Jay's Favorite Chocolate
    Cupcakes, 70
  Peanut Butter and Jelly
    Cupcakes, 52
  Peanut Butter Chip Cupcakes,
    53
  Peanut Butter Cupcakes, 51
  Vanilla Peanut Butter Cup
    Cupcakes, 54
Peanut Butter Fudge Frosting,
    170
  Chocolate Peanut Butter
    Cupcakes, 19
  Peanut Butter Cupcakes, 51
Pears
  Apple Crisp Cupcakes (v), 30
Pecans
  Candied Pecan Cupcakes, 48
  Coconut Pecan Frosting, 154
  Vegan Carrot Raisin Cupcakes
    (v), 129
  Vegan Pumpkin Pecan
    Cupcakes, 144
Peppermint Candy Cupcakes, 83
Pimm's Cupcakes, 60
Piña Colada Cupcakes, 40
Pineapples
  Carrot Cupcakes, 93
  Piña Colada Cupcakes, 40
  Pineapple Cupcakes, 41
  Tropical Cupcakes (v), 43
Pink Lemonade Cupcakes, 88
Pistachio Cupcakes, 55
Plums
  Cardamom Plum Cupcakes, 92
Poppy seeds
  Almond Poppy Seed Cupcakes,
    49
  Cherry Almond Poppy Seed
    Cupcakes, 34
  Lemon Buttermilk Cupcakes
    (v), 46
  Vegan Almond Cupcakes (v),
    128
Pretty in Pink Cupcakes, 87
Princess Cupcakes, 120
Pumpkin
  Pumpkin Cupcakes, 98

Vegan Pumpkin Pecan
Cupcakes, 144

R

Raisins
Applesauce Cupcakes (v), 102
Carrot Cupcakes (v), 93
Chocolate Gingerbread
Cupcakes, 20
Ginger Cupcakes (v), 96
Hot Fudge Sauce (v), 163
Maple Raisin Cupcakes, 97
Pumpkin Cupcakes (v), 98
Rum Raisin Cupcakes, 67
Sherry Apricot Cupcakes (v),
66
Spice Cupcakes, 99
Vegan Carrot Raisin Cupcakes,
129
Vegan Oat Spice Cupcakes (v),
143
Vegan Pumpkin Pecan
Cupcakes (v), 144
Raspberries
Blueberry Rose Cupcakes, 42
Chocolate Raspberry Cupcakes,
21
Princess Cupcakes (v), 120
Raspberry Vanilla Cupcakes,
107
Vegan Chocolate Raspberry
Cupcakes, 135
Vegan Sweet Vanilla Cupcakes
(v), 145
Rum
Apricot Rum Cupcakes, 31
Hot Fudge Sauce, 163
Rum Buttercream, 171
Rum Raisin Cupcakes, 67
Tropical Cupcakes, 43
White Cupcakes with Coconut
Frosting, 116
Rum Buttercream, 171
Apricot Rum Cupcakes, 31
Blueberry Apricot Cupcakes, 33
Coconut Cupcakes, 82
Mango Coconut Cupcakes, 37
Piña Colada Cupcakes, 40
Pineapple Cupcakes, 41
Rum Raisin Cupcakes, 67
Sherry Apricot Cupcakes, 66
Tropical Cupcakes, 43

S

Salt, about, 14
Sauces. See also Fillings; Glazes;
Toppings
Chocolate Toffee Sauce, 153
Hot Fudge Sauce, 163
Sesame seeds
Toasted Sesame Cupcakes, 118
toasting, 118

Vegan Toasted Sesame
Cupcakes, 146
Sherry
Pumpkin Cupcakes, 98
Sherry Apricot Cupcakes, 66
S'more Cupcakes, 110
Sour cream
Cappuccino Cupcakes, 69
Cheesecake Cupcakes, 112
Chocolate Cheesecake
Cupcakes, 114
Lemon Cheesecake Cupcakes,
113
Rum Buttercream, 171
Soy milk
Vegan Almond Cupcakes, 128
Vegan Carrot Raisin Cupcakes,
129
Vegan Cherry Almond
Cupcakes, 130
Vegan Chocolate Cupcakes, 131
Vegan Chocolate Fudge
Frosting, 177
Vegan Chocolate Orange
Cupcakes, 132
Vegan Chocolate Peppermint
Cupcakes, 134
Vegan Chocolate Raspberry
Cupcakes, 135
Vegan Cinnamon Almond
Cupcakes, 136
Vegan Coconut Cupcakes, 137
Vegan Creamsicle Cupcakes,
139
Vegan Fluffy Lemon Cream
Frosting, 179
Vegan Fluffy Vanilla Cream
Frosting, 183
Vegan Large Batch Frosting, 180
Vegan Lemon Cupcakes, 141
Vegan Oat Spice Cupcakes, 143
Vegan Peanut Butter Frosting,
182
Vegan Pumpkin Pecan
Cupcakes, 144
Vegan Sweet Vanilla Cupcakes,
145
Vegan Toasted Sesame
Cupcakes, 146
Spice Cupcakes, 99
Spiced Peach Cupcakes, 101
Spices, about, 14
Sprinkles
Confetti Cupcakes, 79
Ice Cream Cone Cupcakes, 78
Sticky Date Cupcakes, 119
Strawberries
Pretty in Pink Cupcakes, 87
Strawberry Cream Cheese
Buttercream, 172
Ice Cream Cone Cupcakes, 78
Pretty in Pink Cupcakes, 87
Very Vanilla Chocolate Chip
Cupcakes, 28

White Cupcakes, 85
Superfine sugar, about, 64

T

Tea
Anise Cupcakes, 90
Chai Cupcakes, 104
Earl Grey Cupcakes, 73
Green Tea Cupcakes, 74
Toasted Sesame Cupcakes, 118
Toffee Cupcakes, 84
Toppings. See also Fillings;
Frostings; Glazes; Sauces
Lemon Cream, 164
Whipped Cream Topping, 175,
Tropical Cupcakes, 43

V

Vanilla Cream Frosting, 160
Apricot Rum Cupcakes, 31
Best Chocolate Cupcakes, 18
Blueberry Apricot Cupcakes, 33
Boston Cream Cupcakes (v), 122
Confetti Cupcakes, 79
Ice Cream Cone Cupcakes, 78
Lemon Yogurt Cupcakes, 45
White Chocolate Chip
Cupcakes, 26
Vanilla Custard Filling, 174
Vanilla Ice Cream, 173
Chocolate Chip Cookie
Cupcakes, 106
Spiced Peach Cupcakes (v), 101
Vanilla paste, about, 28
Coffee Ice Cream, 156
Boston Cream Cupcakes, 122
Easy Buttercream Frosting (v),
159
Vanilla Cream Frosting, 160
Vanilla Custard Filling, 174
Vanilla Ice Cream, 173
Vegan Fluffy Vanilla Cream
Frosting, 183
Vegan Large Batch Frosting, 180
Very Vanilla Chocolate Chip
Cupcakes, 28
Vanilla Peanut Butter Cup
Cupcakes, 54
Vegan
Vegan Almond Cupcakes, 128
Vegan Carrot Raisin Cupcakes,
129
Vegan Cherry Almond
Cupcakes, 130
Vegan Chocolate Cherry
Cupcakes, 126
Vegan Chocolate Cinnamon
Cupcakes, 127
Vegan Chocolate Cupcakes,
131
Vegan Chocolate Fudge
Frosting, 177

Vegan Chocolate Icing, 176
Vegan Chocolate Orange
    Cupcakes, 132
Vegan Chocolate Peppermint
    Cupcakes, 134
Vegan Chocolate Raspberry
    Cupcakes, 135
Vegan Cinnamon Almond
    Cupcakes, 136
Vegan Coconut Cupcakes, 137
Vegan Coffee Cupcakes, 138
Vegan Cream Cheese Frosting,
    184
Vegan Creamsicle Cupcakes, 139
Vegan Fluffy Almond Cream
    Frosting, 178
Vegan Fluffy Vanilla Cream
    Frosting, 183
Vegan Green Tea Matcha
    Cupcakes, 140
Vegan Large Batch Frosting, 180
Vegan Lemon Cupcakes, 141
Vegan Lemon Glaze, 181
Vegan Mocha Cupcakes, 142
Vegan Peanut Butter Frosting,
    182
Vegan Oat Spice Cupcakes, 143
Vegan Pumpkin Pecan
    Cupcakes, 144
Vegan Sweet Vanilla Cupcakes,
    145
Vegan Toasted Sesame
    Cupcakes, 146
Vegan Chocolate Fudge Frosting,
    177
Vegan Almond Cupcakes, 128
Vegan Cherry Almond
    Cupcakes, 130
Vegan Chocolate Cherry
    Cupcakes, 126
Vegan Chocolate Cinnamon
    Cupcakes, 127
Vegan Chocolate Cupcakes, 131
Vegan Chocolate Orange
    Cupcakes, 132
Vegan Chocolate Peppermint
    Cupcakes, 134
Vegan Chocolate Raspberry
    Cupcakes, 135
Vegan Coconut Cupcakes, 137
Vegan Coffee Cupcakes, 138
Vegan Creamsicle Cupcakes,
    139
Vegan Mocha Cupcakes, 142
Vegan Oat Spice Cupcakes, 143
Vegan Sweet Vanilla Cupcakes,
    145
Vegan Cream Cheese Frosting,
    184
Vegan Carrot Raisin Cupcakes,
    129
Vegan Chocolate Cupcakes, 131
Vegan Chocolate Orange
    Cupcakes, 132

Vegan Chocolate Peppermint
    Cupcakes, 134
Vegan Chocolate Raspberry
    Cupcakes, 135
Vegan Cinnamon Almond
    Cupcakes, 136
Vegan Coconut Cupcakes, 137
Vegan Coffee Cupcakes, 138
Vegan Green Tea Matcha
    Cupcakes, 140
Vegan Lemon Cupcakes, 141
Vegan Oat Spice Cupcakes, 143
Vegan Pumpkin Pecan
    Cupcakes, 144
Vegan Sweet Vanilla Cupcakes,
    145
Vegan Toasted Sesame
    Cupcakes, 146
Vegan Fluffy Almond Cream
    Frosting, 178
Vegan Almond Cupcakes, 128
Vegan Cherry Almond
    Cupcakes, 130
Vegan Chocolate Cupcakes, 131
Vegan Chocolate Raspberry
    Cupcakes, 135
Vegan Cinnamon Almond
    Cupcakes, 136
Vegan Sweet Vanilla Cupcakes,
    145
Vegan Toasted Sesame
    Cupcakes, 146
Vegan Fluffy Lemon Cream
    Frosting, 179
Vegan Lemon Cupcakes, 141
Vegan Sweet Vanilla Cupcakes,
    145
Vegan Fluffy Vanilla Cream
    Frosting, 183
Vegan Almond Cupcakes, 128
Vegan Carrot Raisin Cupcakes,
    129
Vegan Cherry Almond
    Cupcakes, 130
Vegan Chocolate Cupcakes, 131
Vegan Cinnamon Almond
    Cupcakes, 136
Vegan Coconut Cupcakes, 137
Vegan Coffee Cupcakes, 138
Vegan Creamsicle Cupcakes,
    139
Vegan Green Tea Matcha
    Cupcakes, 140
Vegan Lemon Cupcakes, 141
Vegan Mocha Cupcakes, 142
Vegan Oat Spice Cupcakes, 143
Vegan Pumpkin Pecan
    Cupcakes, 144
Vegan Sweet Vanilla Cupcakes,
    145
Vegan Toasted Sesame
    Cupcakes, 146
Vegan Lemon Glaze, 181
Cranberry Lemon Cupcakes, 35

Lemon Yogurt Cupcakes, 45
Pimm's Cupcakes, 60
Pink Lemonade Cupcakes, 88
Vegan Peanut Butter Frosting,
    182
Vegan Sweet Vanilla Cupcakes,
    145
Vegan Chocolate Cupcakes, 131
Very Vanilla Chocolate Chip
    Cupcakes, 28

W

Walnuts
    Malted Espresso Cupcakes (v),
        68
    Vegan Carrot Raisin Cupcakes
        (v), 129
Whipped Cream Frosting, 175
    Awesome Almond Cupcakes, 50
    Blueberry Rose Cupcakes, 42
    Cherry Almond Poppy Seed
        Cupcakes, 34
    Margarita Cupcakes, 64
    Princess Cupcakes, 120
White chocolate, about 12, 26
    Espresso Dark Brownie
        Cupcakes (v), 72
    White Chocolate Macadamia
        Cupcakes, 58
White chocolate chips
    Apricot Rum Cupcakes (v), 31
    Chai Cupcakes (v), 104
    Cheesecake Cupcakes (v), 112
    Chocolate Brownie Cupcakes
        (v), 24
    Chocolate Chile Cupcakes (v),
        94
    German Chocolate Cupcakes,
        (v), 18
    Green Tea Cupcakes (v), 74
    Toasted Sesame Cupcakes (v),
        118
    White Chocolate Chip
        Cupcakes, 26
    White Chocolate Macadamia
        Cupcakes, 58
White Cupcakes, 85
    Ice Cream Cone Cupcakes, 78
White Cupcakes with Coconut
    Frosting, 116

Y

Yogurt
    Lemon Yogurt Cupcakes, 45

Z

Zucchini
    Carrot Zucchini Cupcakes,
        117
    Zucchini Chocolate Spice
        Cupcakes, 100